21 Peaceful Nurses

Essays on a Spiritually Guided Practice

To Benté with love!

Edited by

Doris J. Popovich

and

Joan Cantwell

Bente, Thought of you when I saw this. Love

Outskirts Press, Inc.
Denver, Colorado

21 Peaceful Nurses
Essays on a Spiritually Guided Practice

Outskirts Press
http://www.outskirtspress.com

ISBN-10: 1-59800-948-6
ISBN-13: 978-1-59800-948-4

Printed in the United States of America

Table of Contents

1. **Angels** **16**
   by Pat Ahern
2. **Healing Arts** **22**
   by Joan Cantwell
3. **Spiritual Fitness for a Balanced Nursing Practice** **28**
   by Amy Crisman
4. **Confidence Grows with Experience** **34**
   by Mindy Daugherty
5. **Who are you? What's it all about?** **40**
   by Sherry Geiger
6. **Keys to Practicing Nursing with a Spiritual Mindset** **46**
   by Renee Gorby
7. **Do All the Good You Can** **52**
   by Katherine Harris
8. **Injections of Joy** **58**
   by Debra Joy Hart
9. **Connecting Experiences for Spiritual Care** **64**
   by Elizabeth Hood
10. **Body, Mind, Spirit** **70**
    by Michele J. Inge
11. **Medicine Buddha** **76**
    by Diana Keyes
12. **Mindfulness Practice and Nursing Praxis: Keys to Wholeness** **82**
    by Diane Lauver

13.	**Eye of the Hurricane** by Eddie Lueken	**90**
14.	**Spirituality in Nursing Education** by Jane Vernon Lutz	**96**
15.	**A Call to Nursing** by Dawn Marino	**102**
16.	**The Spiral of Healing: Ancient Healing and Modern Medicine** by Loretta D. Melancon	**108**
17.	**Conscious Intention Toward a More Peaceful Life** by Doris Popovich	**114**
18.	**Nursing as a Spiritual Path** by Patrice Rancour	**120**
19.	**Epiphany** by Sarah Seybold	**126**
20.	**Everything Happens for a Reason** by Teresa A. Shuff	**132**
21.	**“Nurse...!”** by Jo Marie Thompson	**138**

Dedications

We dedicate this book to our loving partners, David Beleckis and Mary Diamond, for their kind and patient support while we were adrift in creativity. Their individual healing journeys and spiritual presence have been our daily inspiration.

Appreciations

Our deepest thanks to our families, friends and colleagues for their friendship, insights, talents and inspiration.

Special Thanks from Doris

Thanks to the Masters, Teachers and Loved Ones, past and present, who continue to hold the light for my creative self, and for this work.

Loving gratitude to my mom, Louise Popovich, who taught me, above all, to let my intuition be my guide.

Special thanks to Joan, my coeditor, for being such a joyful, ego-free collaborator. This project truly has been a pleasure!

I'd also like to thank Whitney Scott, editor extraordinaire, for the enduring impact she has had on my development as a writer.

Special thanks to our proofreaders: Mary Diamond, Meta Hellman, and Eileen Kozak. We couldn't have done it without you.

Thanks also to my writing group – Carol, Meta, Loraine, Pat and Deb – for helping to keep hope alive, and for teaching me to live the writer's life, whether or not I was writing.

Special Thanks from Joan

To Tom and Marie Cantwell, my parents, who have nurtured and supported my creativity since childhood.

Doris Popovich, my classmate and co-editor, whose, vision, inspiration and optimism for this project are living proof of the power of creative manifestation.

Special thanks to my teachers: Carol LaChapelle, for your patience and ongoing encouragement as I struggled over the years to find my authentic voice. To Rev. Patricia Novick, for showing me the sacredness in everything, and to Lucia Capacchione, Ph.D., A.T.R., for giving me the creative tools that enabled me to reinvent my life.

And finally, to Jean Kemnitz for your timeless friendship and to Leslie Shiel for your support, artistic vision and poetic spirit.

Preface

In October 2004 we each received an invitation to our 25-year nursing school reunion. It seemed impossible that 25 years had passed since our graduation from Wesley-Passavant School of Nursing, in Chicago. Over the years we had lost touch with each other. The reunion offered us a chance to rekindle our friendship; to reminisce about the rigors of nursing school, and to laugh about all the fun we managed to have. Naturally, we also began to reflect on how the nursing profession had changed.

The topic of the current nursing shortage and subsequent low morale among nurses was unavoidable. We had each held rewarding and challenging positions over the years, and we began to share with each other our souls' secrets to professional success, as well as our personal strategies for staying sane! Spiritual fitness was a common thread in our stories. We decided, after not too long a conversation, that we were both very wise women. And, we were struck by how much help we had received over the years from our peers - our masters, mentors and teachers. We agreed that there was much wisdom within our profession, wisdom that, when shared, might alter the temporary condition of low morale. We wanted to know if other nurses relied on spiritual truths to get them through the stress inherent in nursing today. This anthology grew out of these questions.

We asked nurses to submit an essay "on the diverse topic of spiritual fitness for a balanced nursing practice". We wanted to get to the "spiritual mysteries of professional success." We sought to understand how nurses sustained themselves spiritually. How they dealt with issues of presence, perseverance, surrender and control. How they avoided burnout? What was the spiritual dimension to our work?

21 Peaceful Nurses is not meant to be a panacea for the complex issues surrounding the nursing profession. It is meant to be a source of hope and inspiration, a way of honoring the spiritual paths of nurses practicing peace in the workplace.

This anthology represents a cross-section of the responses we received. We send special thanks to the many fabulous nurses who submitted essays for consideration. We know now, without a doubt, that today's nurses are a wise assembly of healers. We hope that your heart will be touched by these 21 peaceful nurses. Our's certainly were!

Blessings,

Doris and Joan

Special Invitation: If you are a nurse, and you have an essay that you would like to submit for publication in 21 Peaceful Nurses, Second Edition, please visit www.mindfullivingproductions.com for complete submission guidelines.

"Imagination is more important than knowledge."

Albert Einstein

1

Angels

Celestial: An attendant or guardian originating from God.

Angels

Pat Ahern

In the early 80's I was absolutely convinced that the only thing standing between life and earth was me: the trusty, capable and vigilant bedside nurse in the CCU. I was like a sharp shooter with all the equipment, fearless and cocky, as only a rookie critical care nurse can be. It was on a typically crazy day in the CCU that we admitted a 60 year old, Mr. D, with an acute MI. He was very sick: cardiogenic shock, on an intra-aortic balloon pump with ventilator. I remember him wiggling his toes and winking at me, as sick as he was. I could see a blue-eyed glittery look that told me if he makes it, he's going to be a real pistol of a patient. He had an adoring family including a daughter who was finishing high school. His wife was steady, sturdy and unwavering. She was a true match for him with steely resolve to come through this assault.

After a few days, Mr. D was well enough to be extubated and removed from the ventilator. He was recovering slowly and steadily when he unexpectedly had a cardiac arrest. I was at his side when he arrested and I was able to successfully apply the defibrillator paddles and reverse his ventricular arrhythmia. Afterward, the doctor asked Mr. D what he remembered about the experience. Mr. D replied that he thought he had died, but when he opened his eyes and saw me with those paddles, he knew he wasn't in heaven and hoped he was not in hell! Some angel I turned out to be! We laughed a lot that day and for the many weeks of his long recovery.

I remember our chaplain saying to me, "How many people go home and say, '*I saved a life today?*'" Thinking about that and, wrapped in my Teflon nurse shield, I laughed it off—just my job, don't you know? But it dawned on me that day that nursing is a profession of art and science, bound together by reverence for life. I began to understand my work as a calling, not a job. And I started to know humility.

Several months later, Mr. D sent me a hand-made Christmas card of an angel that looked a lot like me except there were bolts of lighting all around me. Mr. D, it turns out, was an accomplished artist. Over the years, I occasionally heard about him and his family, until I left my position at the hospital and we lost touch.

Flash forward more than twenty years and I am the CEO of a very different care environment, Rainbow Hospice. Now I know that I have found the perfect blend of art and science nursing: end-of-life care. My calling has been transformed into supporting and leading the nurses and other staff that provide tender, gentle care to people who are dying. Now I am absolutely convinced that there is nothing standing between life and death. Death is a life experience. I have an intense desire to achieve the very best work environment for my amazing staff, and therefore, to influence the quality of care that they can provide to our patients, families and bereaved clients.

A call comes, and it is Mr. D's daughter, now a nurse. She talks about the formative witnessing of the care her dad received from me 20 years ago, as her call to nursing. I am deeply touched. She tells me about her parents: her dad is now dying and needs hospice. Mom is taking care of him at home—still unwavering in her resolve but weary and alert to the needs she has for herself as well as her family. She needs fortification.

I am struck by the fact that this family survived a sudden near-death, only now to experience a long decline from cancer. The daughter assures me that her dad made the best of every single day he had. Many times over the years he talked about his gift of time and how grateful he was to have been resuscitated. But now, he loves his home, his privacy, his view of Lake Michigan, and his pets and he wants to die in his own bed. Mostly, he wants to be with his family, surrounded by the people and things he loves. He wants to hold the hand of his bride at the end.

Mr. D has told his family that the last time he died, I got in the way and he was so glad I did. He had so many more years of living left. But now, he hopes that I will help him feel safe and prepared for the death he is now ready to experience. He knows that it is the same Patty Ahern taking care of him in two very different circumstances, and he is glad to know me again. Even though I do not visit him, I feel those glittery steel-blue eyes upon me.

Rainbow Hospice did admit Mr. D and he lived for several months, always in his condo with his wife and family—looking out on the lake he loved, especially at sunrise. I had a few opportunities to talk with his family and I was able to stay in touch with him vicariously, through the wonderful Rainbow nurse providing his care. I took such comfort in knowing the full-circle of Mr. D's life and the part that I had played in it.

At Mr. D's funeral mass, I felt him winking down at me saying, "This time was the right time" and "Thank you for being the one who made all the difference the first time."

Pat Ahern, RN, MBA
President/Executive Director, Rainbow Hospice

"Learn to breathe through your mouth and speak with your eyes."

Patricia Ahern has served non-profit community-based Rainbow Hospice since 1996. She has a background in managing delivery of patient-care services and in managing change initiatives for such health care organizations as Catholic Health Partners, St. Joseph Health Centers and Hospital, and St. Francis Hospital of Evanston.

She earned her MBA from North Park University, Chicago; her bachelor's degree from Northwestern University, Chicago and her diploma in nursing from St. Francis Hospital, Evanston. She received a certificate in Managing Organizational Change in 1992 from Organizational Development Resources, Inc., and has served as an adjunct faculty member at Lake Forest Graduate School of Business. Currently she serves on the Governance Committee of the National Hospice and Palliative Care Organization, the Board of Directors of the Illinois State Hospice Organization and has been a Rotarian since 1998.

2

Creativity

Originality and Expressiveness: Artistic Imagination

Healing Arts

Joan Cantwell

I first made the connection between creativity and healing 26 years ago at Khao-I-Dang refugee camp. I was a 22-year-old charge nurse working in a 100-bed adult acute care hospital on the Thai-Cambodian border. The camp was inundated with traumatized Cambodian refugees fleeing a civil war and genocide to seek shelter in the international medical relief camps.

During the war, Cambodians had been forced to live in a Maoist, agrarian society. Families were separated and sent to work camps. People were killed if they were literate or had any association with western culture. They were not allowed to practice any art or religion or read or write. Many feigned ignorance, suppressed their knowledge, and threw away their books and reading glasses to stay alive.

The first time I worked night shift alone, the hospital was full with refugees and their family members. One patient had active meningococcal meningitis, and I didn't have an emergency kit. It was just me, a Cambodian assistant, and a doctor on call from another relief hospital in a different part of camp who spoke only French. My medical orders that night were translated from English to Khmer (Cambodian) to French then back again. Our patient needed IV antibiotics and powerful steroids for treatment. Because of the language barriers, we used drawings to illustrate what his medical treatment would be. We did not need language that night; the drawings proved to be a simple, effective method of communication.

Art was more than just a convenient communication tool; it was also a way of healing. In the shelter of the camp, people's spirits came alive as they were finally able to creatively express themselves: played music, danced their indigenous dances, practiced religion, and made art. People picked up crayons or pencils for the first time in years and spontaneously drew or painted their stories of survival, stories that had been held hostage in the refugees' bodies, minds and souls for years.

There was an explosion of art: images documenting heroic escapes from Cambodia and years of torture in prisoner work camps; drawings of family members butchered by Khmer Rouge soldiers; cartoons of starving people working in rice patties with fat soldiers taking their food; paintings of beloved lost family members, and watercolors of destroyed sacred temples. Each image was a portal for documenting the unspeakable and for memorializing the dead.

After returning from Thailand I continued my nursing practice only to later find myself entering into my own healing process from severe "burnout." This included working with a Jungian analyst, taking art and writing classes, and learning powerful centering techniques like mindfulness meditation. As a child, I was always creating: drawing, making papier mache masks, candles, jewelry and collages. I would hole up in our basement for hours, away from the chaos of school and a family of nine, to just do art. When I entered nursing school, I repressed the creative side of me, but years later it came back disguised as burnout and screaming for attention.

I took one painting class at the Art Institute, and like the refugees, I began discovering a new vocabulary for working with my emotions. Then I took a drawing class, then another painting class, then another. With each class, I felt my soul returning. Art was my antidote to depression; it moved me from surviving to thriving. I could once again see creative possibilities for my life.

Art has sustained me for the past twenty-seven years. The type of art I do varies on any given day. Some days I draw, paint, make a collage, write in my journal, or read a poem.

Some days, I just look at art. Whatever form it takes, art is a non-negotiable part of my life.

Since that first art class, I have transformed my nursing career. My experience includes, ICU, maternal / child health, community health, health promotion and wellness, and now hospice and teaching. I integrate the arts into my current nursing practice, providing services that merge the worlds of art and science. Candice Pert in her book *Molecules of Emotion* documents through research the profound connection between our mind and body. We now know that when the ability to express is suppressed it can have severe consequences for people, often manifesting in physical, emotional and spiritual diseases. Art therapy is based on the theory that the creative process has healing effects. When we express what matters to us, both our emotional and physical health improves.

I could have left the nursing profession; I chose instead to reinvent it. I have created my life so that I can be an artist, a nurse and a healer. Art is integrated into every aspect of my work. I now teach expressive arts at several Chicagoland universities and I provide expressive art services to hospice patients. On a recent patient visit, a well-traveled professor of geography with early Alzheimer's disease and I made a collage of all the places in the world he had lived. After looking over pictures of China, India, Hawaii, and Japan he smiled and said, "I had forgotten what a great career I had. What a spectacular life!"

The refugees taught me that it is possible to creatively move beyond one's history, whether that history is surviving the battlefields of Cambodia, our medical system, or the rigors of everyday life. Art heals. It unravels suffering, validates our life experiences, and leads us back to our humanity.

In memory of Haing Ngor, who survived the "Killing Fields" and became an international example of peace and creativity in action.

Joan Cantwell, RN, MA, CJEA
Principal, Mindful Living Productions

"You are born with a creative spirit capable of moving you toward wholeness. Learn to listen to it. It can transform your life."

Joan is a nurse, artist, writer and expressive arts teacher. She provides expressive arts services for patients at Horizon Hospice in Chicago, teaches Introduction to Art Therapy at Roosevelt, DePaul and Dominican Universities, and consults in health and wellness.

Prior to founding Mindful Living Productions, Joan was manager of an award-winning Health and Wellness Program at a Chicago-based Fortune 500 company. She has 25 years experience in comprehensive health care management as well as international and domestic nursing. Joan recently exhibited at The National Vietnam Veterans Art Museum.

3

Moment

Instant: *present time-particle sufficient to turn the scales.*

Spiritual Fitness for a Balanced Nursing Practice

Amy Crisman

You never expect the atomic bomb to land in your own backyard. Over five years ago it landed in mine, leaving a hole so vast it could have left me bereft of my nursing practice forever; even my sanity was at risk. I absolutely loved my job of 10 years as a pediatric oncology nurse in the clinic at Children's Hospital San Diego. Then my infant nephew was diagnosed with JMML, a very rare and potentially lethal form of childhood leukemia.

I'd just lost a baby of my own when I was 16 weeks pregnant. I was not yet over any of the wrenching, desperate heartache that had ensued when this next calamity happened. The stress, fatigue, sleeplessness, hormonal imbalance, alcohol use, and grief at the time threw my neurotransmitters into overdrive. I sustained a nervous breakdown of modestly epic proportions with the diagnosis of bipolar disorder bestowed upon me like a crown of thorns. I went on leave to rest and heal—would I be able to return?

My darling nephew underwent a stem cell transplant and is now a very active six-year-old boy who loves Spiderman and swimming—an enormous miracle. And I call it no small miracle that I was able to return to my nursing practice and continue to be an effective nurse with my very own unique blend of compassion, skill, and humor.

The key for me *is* balance. Equilibrium is essential in maintaining my overall health and is what keeps me prepared to come back to work—again and again, despite our tough patient population and demanding setting. When all aspects of my life are harmonious, without the stressful dissonance that occurs when things are off kilter, then I am more productive and satisfied in my nursing practice, which leads, if you will, to spiritual fitness. The following is what works for me; perhaps something here will resonate with you:

Learn to Say No. When too much stacks up on your plate, it is impossible to do a good job at any of it. Pare down. Ask yourself: Is this activity/committee/incentive shift, etc. something I really, really want to do? If it is, and it will not wear you out, go for it. If it's not, pass on it. Learning that the show will go on without you is one of the most freeing lessons there is. The show might be a little different, but sometimes that's not such a bad thing. I co-lead a support group for adolescents with cancer called SOMBFAB, or Some of My Best Friends Are Bald. I passed on the February meeting because I wasn't feeling well. My co-leaders ran with it. Apparently, it was one of the best (and loudest) meetings we've had in a long time.

Find Your Bliss. For me it's my family—my funny, dear husband of almost twenty years; my witty, amazing, affectionate 16 year old son, and my gift—my youngest boy who is five now, coming along after all the misery and helping all of us heal with his exuberant joy. It's also Padres baseball, Chargers football, writing (something I'd like to do more of), reading—sitting on my porch watching flowers that my husband lovingly planted tremble in the gentle breeze—reminding me that beauty is all around.

Consider Your Habits. Damn it! It's true! Exercise helps. It really does. So does healthy eating and getting enough rest.

Bad habits? Mine was drinking. When good things happened at work, it was a reason to drink. Oh, yeah, bad things too. Pretty soon everything was a reason to drink. I knew I needed to quit so I did—should you? Is there something else you need to look at?

Count Your Blessings. The extraordinary children I work with have taught me to take nothing for granted and to find the best that every day has to offer. These are kids completing brightly colored art projects in the waiting room prior to treatment—and looking forward to the prize box upon completion of it. They are happy to be able to eat without nausea, to walk without pain, to go to school. One child, who was going home on hospice, told me that he was lucky because he'd never been stung by a bee.

Keep the Faith. Whatever yours is. Work it. Pray it. Believe it. Heaven is very real to me. I have worked with young hearts that have seen it.

Be Kind to Each Other. Nurses can eat Meow Mix for breakfast and be catty all day. Be good to your colleagues. Celebrate the different gifts each brings to the table. And when you can't celebrate? Tolerate. There have been times in my career when I was borne aloft on the wings of my co-workers. Without their kindness and love, I know I couldn't continue this challenging work that I cherish.

Remain In the Moment. Most importantly, in addition to the above, how do I sustain a fulfilling nursing practice given all the stressors and demands therein? The answer is simple: moment by moment. If I can make whatever moment I am in with whatever family I am caring for a better moment, one where perhaps the child laughs and the parents' faces relax and I know I have delivered good safe care, then I know I have given that family the best moment possible. At the end of the day, I have strung together a handful of moments and I can go home feeling content: I have made a good difference in my patients' lives. And at the end of my career, I can look forward to looking back over an immeasurable series of moments—moments that made up a professional lifetime of giving the best I had to offer and the grace that will come with knowing I did.

Amy Crisman, RN, BSN, CPON
(Certified Pediatric Oncology Nurse)

"Initially in a moment of immobilizing frustration, I close my eyes and say a silent prayer. I narrow the time focus down to attend to the immediate task at hand, even breaking that down into steps if necessary. I always keep in the back of my mind that at the end of the day I will finish and go home! And when I do, I celebrate my family, especially my children."

Amy Crisman completed her Bachelor's of Nursing at University of California Los Angeles in 1985. Her first nursing job was at Rancho Park Hospital, a small private psychiatric hospital for adolescents. In 1987 she became a staff nurse at Children's Hospital and Health Center San Diego, working inpatient with mainly oncology patients. Shortly thereafter, she was hired in the Outpatient Hematology-Oncology Clinic. Amy is co-director of a peer support group for adolescents with cancer entitled SOMBFAB, or Some of My Best Friends Are Bald. The group will celebrate its sixteenth birthday in October. She lives with her husband of almost 20 years, and two wonderful boys, Kellen, age 16 and Sean, age five.

4

Faith

Trust: *fidelity to one's promises.*

Confidence Grows with Experience

Mindy Daugherty

My nursing instructors always said, "Confidence grows with experience - fake it 'til you make it."

A well known Comanche healer woman, named Sanapia, was born in 1895. At the age of 14, with encouragement from her mother and grandmother, she accepted her call to become a healer and began her training. She studied plants and herbs and learned to identify and apply them in the healing ways of her ancestors.

When Sanapia was 17, her training included a ritual ceremony where hot coals were placed in her hands. These coals did not give her the sensation of pain but rather an exhilarating chill—rushing up her arms and thus carrying with it the gift of healing. Then, her mother transmitted power to her mouth by brushing two eagle feathers past her open lips. From then on, Sanapia would carry in her mouth a curative spirit called Medicine Eagle.

The whirl of six different IV pumps humming along at once never seems comforting to me. These pumps are lifelines connecting my patient to powerful drugs. One small adjustment either way could cure or kill. The mass of tubing looks like spaghetti next to his pasty-white head. Chest tubes suck blood from around his heart and into a drainage box at the foot of the bed. Urine runs down a tube into a bag hanging on the bedrail…hopefully. Another tube goes into his throat forcing precise volumes of air into his lungs. Other wires monitor every possible pressure in his heart and vasculature.

The numbers and waveforms on the monitors, the color and temperature of the skin, the effects of medicines going in and the amounts of drainage coming out—they all add up to this patient's outcome. Modern medicine. This is how healing has evolved.

Sanapia was instructed to spend four nights alone on the mountaintop as part of her training to become a great healer. Her elders warned her that her courage might be tested on one of those nights by dark spirits trying to wrestle away her medicine. Fearing the dark spirits, Sanapia fled the mountain at dusk each of the four evenings and spent those nights curled up beneath the front porch of her house.

I am alone with my patient in a small recovery room for the first crucial hours after his surgery. There are no windows. The fluorescent lights scream artificial insults at me. The only colors in the room are those of body fluids: red, yellow and green. No family or clergy is allowed in until I am sure he is fairly stabilized. All the patient hears is my voice, and my instructions to be calm and everything will be OK. I say the same words of comfort to every patient. It must sound like a tape-recorded message by now.

I think of the body as a machine only in this setting. This is an area of nursing that requires complete confidence and emotionless skill. You cannot let rapid hemorrhage or the ceasing of a heartbeat affect you or you will fail. You become a machine like the body in the bed. Medicine used to be more of an art.

Sanapia could not cure everyone who came to her and she was aware of the limits of her powers. She attributed these difficulties to not having stood up to the dark mountain spirits. Even so, her importance to her community went well beyond the numbers she cured and comforted. To her tribespeople,

Sanapia was living proof of the real and enduring power of all Comanche healers who came before her.

My patient's wife steps through the sliding door and into the bright square box of a room. She slides her chair next to him and looks at me with a tear slipping from her eye. I nod my head with permission and smile at her. She places her hand in her husband's and bends down to kiss his wrinkled forehead. He opens his eyes for the first time and weakly smiles around the breathing tube. His chances of survival have now improved.

Mindy Daugherty, RN, CLNC

"I remember that the world still turns and life goes on when the frustration gets overwhelming."

Mindy Daugherty has been a registered nurse for 13 years. She has practiced in the areas of critical care, home care, long term care and hospice. She is currently working as a legal nurse consultant. Mindy is married with three children.

5

Purpose

Aim: *something set up as an object or end to be attained.*

"Who are you?" What's it all about?

Sherry Geiger

If you watch the TV series, *CSI*, you may or may not recognize the show's theme music: *"Who Are You?"* recorded by the popular sixties rock group called *The Who*. I believe that knowing who we are and how we relate to others is essential to "living (well) in the moment" and gaining insight into the meaning of our very existence. My personal quest for spiritual wisdom begins with considering how the nurse part of me impacts who I am and how I relate to others.

I became a registered nurse after graduating in 1967. I entered nursing directly from high school in 1964. It was a time when there were few career options for women other than secretary, teacher, or nurse. These professions were what you did while waiting for your Prince Charming to sweep you off your feet and give you a nice home and lovely children.

I fell in love with the *idea* of becoming a nurse while delivering dinner trays to patients in our local hospital when I was still in high school. I loved the nurses' crisp white uniforms and caps, white stockings, and even their sensible, no nonsense shoes. I most admired their ability to organize and meet a myriad of responsibilities while still finding time to do the small things that brought comfort, reassurance and greater understanding to anxious patients and families. For me, the hospital was a magical community that exemplified all that is best about human beings, a place where people worked together and helped those who were humbled if not frightened by disease, aging, or some unknown infirmity.

I still enjoy the challenge of being part of solving that magic, becoming an instrument of healing, of serving and loving others. I suspect that I learned those ideals from my family and from church teachings that were central in my early life. I left organized religion when I was 39. I attribute that change in part to gaining a broader concept of God as developed through experiences with diverse patients and developing more knowledge of and respect for a variety of cultures and religions. I believe my current understanding of God makes Him truly omnipotent and even more loving than the God I learned to love as a child.

Over the past 38 years I have worked in Labor and Delivery, Med-Surg, Acute Care Psychiatry, cancer research, prenatal and immunization clinics, school nursing with severe behavior handicapped and multi-handicapped students, and currently as a gerontological nurse for home care. Each of these roles has brought expanded knowledge and new skills for living as well as allowing me to witness many of the divine mysteries of life. I've seen many joyful births and the pain of stillbirth or anomaly. I've rejoiced with those who have overcome deep depressions and psychotic breaks as well as wept with staff and families when those who appeared to be getting well, ended their own lives while out on hospital pass or shortly following hospital discharge. As a school nurse I was challenged and often frustrated working with parents who had little time or apparent interest in their children. At the same time, I was awed by families who, despite all odds, were providing special needs children with endless patience, love, and exceptional care 24/7…year after year. On the cancer research unit I was part of technologically advanced care that returned patients to active, productive lives. I held the hands of young and old, as they lay dying. Knowing why I became a nurse tells me a bit about what my family and church taught me about myself and about the world. Choosing to continue to be a nurse affirms those same values and explains the core of who I am.

Nursing can be very challenging work that requires considerable energy. It's work, however, that allows me to grow in love for humanity and for myself. "If you love everything, you will perceive the divine mystery in things. Once you perceive it, you will begin to comprehend it better every day, and you will come at last to love the whole world with an all-embracing love" (Fyodor Dostoyevsky). This quote has special meaning for me as a nurse because I believe *we* work in a milieu where there is frequent human and divine interplay.

Nursing gives me a sense of purpose and fulfillment. What other profession could offer such diversity and breadth of experience? How many jobs could hone such practical everyday life skills that make us better sons, daughters, mothers, fathers, neighbors? There are days when my job is less than rewarding and I sometimes speculate on the road not taken, a different career, but ultimately I have resolved that nursing for me is the means to "have come at last to love the whole world with an all-embracing love," and I am happy with who I am and my small place in the world.

Sherry Geiger, RN,C

"You must continually nurture your own brain, body and spirit if you expect to be able to give the same good guidance to your patients."

Sherry Geiger, RN,C graduated from The Christ Hospital in Cincinnati OH, a residential three-year diploma school which will soon become The Christ College. She has worked full or part time, in hospitals and in public health for 38 years. She and husband, Bruce, have three daughters, two grandchildren, and always at least one dog.

6

Dedication

Given Over: *commitment to a goal or way of life.*

Keys to Practicing Nursing with a Spiritual Mindset

Renee Gorby

With the current nursing shortage looming and increased attention to the "bottom line" by hospital administrators, it is increasingly imperative that nurses return to their roots, and concentrate on the basics of our profession. If we approach our tasks with the awareness that our patients are first and foremost persons of worth, who are generally striving to do the best they can under the circumstances, then we connect with them as people. And, as people, more often than not, we can reach common ground. Our challenges, in trying to do more with less, a phrase I am told regularly to implement, are becoming strained. In the process of trying to do all it is that we must do, including the immense documentation requirements from which the dollars flow, we can lose track of both the patient who is entrusted to our care, and of ourselves, and the unique and privileged position we have as caretakers. In our role, we come into contact with people and their families, most likely, in times of crisis. These crises range from personal tragedies, such as the teenager involved in a serious motor vehicle accident, to moments of hope, for example, when a young couple is first presented their newborn and all the awe in that moment.

I have been blessed with the opportunity to be a part of patients' lives for the past 24 years. During this time, I have tried hard to not lose sight of the goal of treating each patient as I would want to be treated myself. I have endeavored to stay aware of the "golden rule" and to be fully present to those I am responsible for, and to give my best each and every day.

At this point in my career, I have a rather lengthy commute to work. I have put into practice a plan of asking God for guidance on my way into work as well as to be a blessing to those I encounter during the day. I have found that sometimes a kind word or deed, however small, makes a big impact. This holds true for both patients and coworkers. On the drive home, I consciously strive to put my workday behind me and to prepare for the evening. For myself, a time of respite and refueling away from the hospital renews my spirit and refreshes me. Then, I am better able to meet the demands tomorrow holds. I truly take a "one day at a time" approach to my position, giving my all each day but being careful not to borrow tomorrow's troubles. I attempt to rededicate my decision to be in my particular job on a regular basis. These small steps adjust my attitude in a positive way. Because I have chosen to be here, in this hospital, at this time, I strive to do my best for my patients and for my coworkers. There exists an empowerment from choosing to continue at my present job, as opposed to being swept along with the tide.

When I come into contact with nursing students, I try to impart words of wisdom to them and help them gain confidence in their role. Their mastery is crucial to their future success. I try to remember my own school days and the way I felt. Empathy for others is key in helping me relate to others in a serene way, one that I would want if I were again in "their shoes."

I also employ this technique of "wearing another's shoes," when I interact with other disciplines on the medical team, whether they are physicians, social workers, or housekeeping staff, trying to have the grace to make requests with courtesy and respect. I find this method of communicating to be "contagious." Being gracious cultivates an environment of further courtesies being extended by coworkers and others we meet during the day.

Our expectations generally come to pass. Given this, I make a point of expecting things to work out, and my experience is that they do. Nursing has been a wonderfully satisfying profession for me. I have been blessed with opportunities to work with a wide variety of patient populations and have been invited to assist people in their moments of deepest need. I cannot imagine a more meaningful way to participate in others' lives.

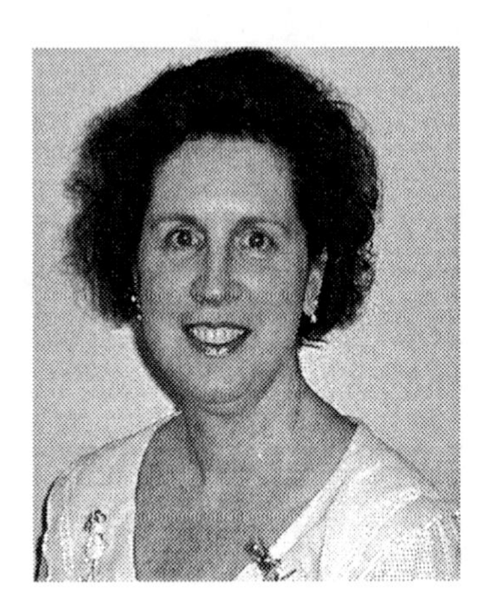

Renee Gorby, RN

"When frustrated, I try to remember that although the mountain top experiences in life are exhilarating and uplifting, they do not represent life in its entirety. It is in the valleys of life that I experience the most growth."

Renee Gorby is a registered nurse with 24 years of experience, from staff nursing to Director of Nursing. She has worked in many inpatient settings from medical/surgical units, psychiatric units, newborn nursery, orthopedics, to ICUs. Renee has also worked outpatient in a pediatric practice and has taught nursing students in their clinical rotations.

7

Willingness

Readiness: *accepting by choice, without reluctance.*

Do All the Good You Can

Katherine Harris

Do all the good you can,
By all the means you can,
In all the ways you can,
In all the places you can,
At all the times you can.

Anonymous.

As a mother and nurse I get to practice compassion in the face of chaos and fear every day.

Before I had children three years ago, I spent a lot of time thinking about my spiritual practice. I went to nourishing yoga classes twice a week and on 10-day silent meditation retreats twice a year. Discipline and serenity were my goals; I thought that with enough focused quiet time, I could create some spiritual progress and become a better person. Then I had a baby, a baby who cried when I didn't hold her. No longer could I be silent in solitude. What replaced the solitude was the very real practice of trying to stay calm and kind when my life was totally altered and I always had a little person in my arms. Luckily, I fell deeply in love with my daughter and saw that I was going to have to change my notion that spiritual practice necessitated separation from everyday life. For guidance I looked to my experience as a labor and delivery nurse. Over the seven years I'd been a nurse I had learned my job was to do all the good I could even as chaos descended, as it often did on a busy, understaffed unit.

I have learned how to do this from watching the best of my

fellow nurses. Over the years I have seen how they treat their patients and me. When I am challenged and stuck I ask, "Who do you want to be?" "What would Terri or Ellie or Kim do in this situation?" Their first instinct is to connect and offer kindness, even to the drug addicted mother who lied to us all about her drug use until her baby started to seize; even to the terrible teenager swearing at us before she's even in labor. I am amazed by the professionalism I see everyday; the midwives and doctors and managers I work with exemplify it as well, but it's the nurses who are in the trenches with me, spending time with the patients and showing me how it's done.

My time to interact with patients is short; they are usually only in the hospital for a couple of days having a baby or gynecological surgery, and once they leave I'll probably never see them again. What I try to do is provide them with good nursing care and compassion. This is my practice. Sometimes I feel lazy and would rather chat with my friends or check my email, but I try to drag myself out of the chair at the end of my shift and offer a backrub to my elderly hysterectomy patient. When I reach out and offer kindness and love, it is rarely refused. We both benefit, I by connecting with another human being, while my patient feels supported and loved in a foreign, often scary, environment.

Recently, I came into work and my assignment was being discussed. One nurse thought I should be given the choice to refuse the patient who had unsuccessfully tried to commit suicide two years ago by setting herself on fire. I was told she didn't look like a person: her face was gone, eyes peeking out unevenly from shiny red skin. When talking to her one didn't know where to look, and drool continuously streamed down her chin. Rarely, if ever, am I given the option to change my assignment. For a moment I considered it. I could have had an easy night with postpartum mothers instead of helping this woman with no fingertips or hair deliver her first child. But of course I took her; that's my job, that's what I do. That's what nurses do. We actually don't get the choice of dealing with the easy and familiar; instead, we are pushed headlong into the difficult, sad, and tragic every week. It's my job to stay focused, offering what I can: good nursing care and compassion. At times like this I am thankful for my experiences doing yoga and meditation. Even though it's been years since my last retreat, I still know how to take a deep breath and be present through painful experiences.

I took the assignment that night and I entered the room with anxiety, but after a few moments I realized, "Oh, she is just a person, just like the rest of us, just like me." She did a beautiful job birthing her baby and by the end of it I felt blessed to be there, blessed to wipe away the drool and tears from her face as she held her chunky newborn boy.

Being a nurse and working with many wonderful nurses has taught me to be brave and to walk into life experiences. If I keep my eyes and heart open, I will learn and be touched. I am more bruised and open, and often there is great sadness, but I feel more alive and connected to the world around me. Maybe in a few years after my second child is weaned I'll be able to go on a meditation retreat, but I don't have to anymore. Everything I need is right in front of me.

Katherine Harris, RN

"To overcome moments of immobilizing frustration I do a lot of deep breathing and a lot of laughing. I remind myself to get through one moment at a time and do the best I can with what I've got."

Katherine Harris is a registered nurse practicing on an OB floor. She lives in New England with her husband and two small children. She has written for The Women's Times, The Hampshire Gazette and Nursing Spectrum.

8

Humor

Laugh: *to produce the sound of, or appearance of joy.*

Injections of Joy

Debra Joy Hart

"There is no room for creativity in this program!" proclaimed my interviewer. I was an art educator applying to nursing school. I was involved in healing touch therapies for 10 years before I ever applied to this program. I saw inventiveness in the dispensation of prayer and miracles. No room for creativity? Who was she kidding? I knew enough to be quiet and not argue with the woman that held my future in her hands. My goal was to be the nurse that gave patients the best of both worlds: traditional and non-traditional therapies. I was accepted into school and thus began the marriage of humor and spirituality, as an adjunct therapy to anything that the mind, body or spirit needed to grow or shed.

Back in the days when we gave shots to each other (OSHA would never stand for that now) I knew my time was coming to receive a two-inch needle in my right gluteal cheek from a fellow nursing student. I began to dream of a 12-foot needle growing longer and longer, looking something like a cross between Pinocchio's nose and a fencing foil. However, that creativity that I was not supposed to use beckoned me. I knew if I made my nurse partner laugh, the imagined saber needle would return to its normal size, no geyser of blood would spring from my butt and no permanent nerve damage would occur. Before the dreaded event, I went to the ladies room and placed several colored smile face stickers (stolen from my five-year-old) on both gluteal cheeks, just in case my needle partner made a wrong turn. When it was my turn to "receive," I paused, politely turned my derrière toward my partner and teacher, dropped my drawers and bent over. Needless to say, the injection was painless for all involved. I learned this important nursing equation: Humor Plus Relaxation Equals Less Pain.

Four years of oncology/hospice/home nursing "back boned" my belief in the marriage of humor and spirituality. Whether people were doing their damnedest to live or their damnedest to die, humor restored their dignity along the way. People who are the receivers of healthcare are constantly "being done to" which in turn promotes the indignity of helplessness. Jocularity restores the balance within the spiritual ecosystem of giving and receiving. Appreciative contributions of wit, winks, and smiles coming from my patients, strengthened my courage to go into the next room, bandage a horrific gaping wound or place a loved one on a morgue cart.

In 1988, HIV/AIDS was on the "Scary Disease List" (official name) put out by the Center for Disease Control (CDC). Fear of the disease was attacking nurses as we did our job. Gallows humor was the light saber that we used to cut through the daily onslaught of the public's ignorance. Many years later, as a hospital clown, rainbow suspenders, red-hearted boxer shorts (which I was always willing to show), a two-foot tall plastic thermometer, a rubber chicken, and plenty of stickers for patients and staff were the new tools in my medicine bag. It didn't matter if I was dressed as a clown or as a nurse, my goal was the same: treat all with injections of joy, dignity and self-esteem.

Humor in nursing is a lot like gardening in a wild prairie. I plant a few seeds of silliness and I never know what will sprout up. Sometimes my tears are the water and my sarcasm is the fertilizer. Words like "We need to be serious" or nurses that seem to be afraid to laugh and condemn those that do, trample the tender seedlings of hope and faith that grow from humor. The beauty of it all is seeing blooming rainbows connect the mind, body and spirit. Burnout in nursing begins when there is no crop of rainbows.

To continue in nursing I have to find new and creative ways to plant within my own garden of giving. I cultivate my garden with the most spiritually potent substances known to humankind: laughter and love. I remember not all strengths are for all plants. I may need a gentle sly smile for a dying man's seemingly wicked joke. I chuckle and snort about bald men with the woman who just lost all her hair. An eight hour shift with substance abuse clients has me questioning the sobriety of life. Having a friend share the bawdiest of jokes over the internet gives me a healthy drink and restores me to a sense of balance. It doesn't drown my sorrows. It refreshes me from the desert of unhealthy behavior.

I look for the silliness and serenity of the body. I am in awe of the daily healing miracles that happen to our mind, body and spirit. I appreciate the good that chemistry can do for the body and I cry and curse the ills it also is capable of. Most of all, I am in awe of the resiliency of the human spirit.

Lastly, I have learned to nourish my nurse soul with this prayer. Called "A Clown's Prayer," it is written by some anonymous clown. When I read it my spirit breathes easier—with or without my clown nose:

"Lord, as I stumble through this life, help me to create more laughter than tears, dispense more happiness than gloom and spread more cheer than despair. Never let me become so indifferent that I fail to see the wonder in the eyes of a child or the twinkle in the eyes of the aged. Never let me forget that my total effort is to cheer people, to make them happy and forget, at least for the moment, all the unpleasant things in their lives. And, Lord, in my final moment, may I hear you whisper, 'When you made my people smile, you made me smile.' "

Debra Joy Hart, RN

"Dear Lord, Please let me give 100% of myself to my nursing profession…15% on Mondays, 25% on Tuesdays, 10% on Wednesdays, 25% on Thursdays, 5% on Fridays and split the remaining 20% if I have to work a weekend shift."

Debra Joy Hart, RN has been in health care for 113 years. Currently she is employed in a substance abuse clinic, and teaches at a local men's transitional/homeless shelter. She also juggles clowning and speaking in corporations, colleges, health care and religious organizations. Her infectious spirit, laughter, and wit are just a few of the tools she has in her clown medicine bag.

Debra was awarded an Honorable Mention for her entry into Mindful Living Production's essay contest, from which this anthology was populated.

9

Listen

Hear: *with thoughtful attention.*

Connecting Experiences for Spiritual Care

Elizabeth Hood

Thinking back, it is hard to pinpoint how and when I started to learn about spiritual care. At first I think we nurses thought that spirituality was the same as religion, and back then you wouldn't dare bring up religion with a patient. Now, I think spirituality is so much bigger than religion. It is not that religion isn't part of spirituality. It is just that, well, everyone, whether they are religious or not, needs to value something and connect meaningfully. I really wanted to learn how to help my patients as best I could. At first I thought we'd be taught what to do or say to fix patients' problems—you know—the right words, the right remedy, the right skill. But I don't remember learning anything in particular about spiritual care back then. Sometimes, I'd feel so blooming lost. One day I saw a woman throw her Bible and shout at her pastor, "God couldn't know!" Later, I cautiously asked what had happened. Not knowing what to say, the best I could do was just listen. She cried and complained about his suggestion that she just had to have more faith. Really, I didn't know what to do, except pass the Kleenex. Amazingly, she *thanked* me! Afterward I wondered: What had I done? What had really made her so angry? What did she need from him that he didn't give?

Thinking about her situation reminded me of losing my own baby. You see, I still blamed myself. I hadn't paid enough attention to ominous symptoms that, as a nurse, I should have known. Like her, I couldn't forgive myself. Although I connected on a personal level with her situation, I had lost faith in myself and didn't think I could do much of anything to help her. Even so, I realized that she appreciated my attention. So, after that, I began making more time to listen to my patients.

Then, years later, on the anniversary of my baby's death, I found myself in the hospital having a hysterectomy. I must have seemed a little off to the nurses. There was no privacy. Late at night a nurse found me hiding in the washroom. I guess she could tell I had been crying. She came right in and closed the door. She asked if I needed to talk. Whatever she said made me trust her, and the floodgates just opened. I told her how I believed I killed my baby, but everyone around me had grown weary of hearing me blame myself. They just wanted me to forget and move on. I felt so guilty. Then, the story of the woman and her Bible came to mind. Like her, I even thought God was punishing me by taking away my womb. Seems kind of incredible now…

But the care of that nurse was different. Not once did she deny that I was responsible. Instead, she listened and listened. Ha, she even helped me rip off some toilet paper for my nose. Then, she crouched down holding my arm while I sat on the toilet blithering and wiping away tears. She was different than me, though. She didn't seem scared at all. She said, "It must be horrible to lose something that is so precious to you and feel so responsible for so long. I've known other women who've told me it is like they also feel dead." She hit the nail right on the head! We talked a bit more about God and those still-raw feelings. I think it was just feeling heard that meant so much. The whole thing was over in about five minutes. But for me, that was the turning point. I think we really connected that night, connected too with others I have nursed in the past. I know, for me, I no longer felt alone with my burden. The lights came on and I was finally able to let go of the guilt. I was probably just another patient to her, but I will never forget what she did. She took a little bit of me and fed it back. This helped me reconnect with the spirit in my life again.

Not only that, when I got back to work, I started to do things a bit differently. I realized how helpful it had been for me to just have somebody to hear me out and not tell me I was wrong. So I made a point of trying to take time to ask my patients what was on their mind each day. Then I'd just listen carefully. I'd try not to judge. It is kind of like the Golden Rule, you know: do unto others how you'd like it done for you. It happened more often on evenings and nights. Sometimes I'd be reminded of my own experience or what other patients had told me. Like that nurse had done with me, I'd share some of those experiences.

There came a point when I realized that I no longer felt like I had to have all the right answers. I didn't need to tell my patients what to do, I just needed to listen and in a small way help them to figure it out for themselves. Sometimes they just needed someone to be there to acknowledge how awful circumstances were for them. Sometimes they'd ask questions about God and stuff that I couldn't answer. Usually I would ask if they wanted me to call pastoral care. However, most times they just needed a few moments of my time to hear them out and help them find their own meaning. Over time, I began to feel closer and closer to my patients and I liked my job better and better.

How I learned about spiritual care, you ask? Basically, I guess, it was through opening, struggling, and connecting so many personal and professional experiences. That was the way through. That's the growth; that's the hope.

Note: Text adapted from Appendix A: Hood, L.E. (2004). Connecting spirituality: How nurses learn to care for the spiritual needs. (Unpublished doctoral dissertation) University of Alberta Faculty of Nursing, Edmonton, AB.

Dr. Elizabeth Hood, RN, PhD

"To work through frustration, I use meditative prayer, therapeutic touch, and a long soak in a bath tub (think tank)."

Dr. Elizabeth Hood holds diplomas and degrees in general nursing, psychiatric nursing, and gerontology. Keenly interested in spirituality and health, she draws on over 30 years of knowledge and experience working in diverse educational and nursing practice settings across Canada and in India. Previous research explored the history, theory, and experience of spirituality in nursing. She developed a spiritual well-being model that can be used to understand and assess the spiritual domain of human health. In recent research, Dr. Hood discovered that nurses use a cyclical, intertwined, and progressive process of opening to, struggling with, and making connections between personal and professional experiences in learning how to care for spiritual needs.

Dr. Hood was awarded an Honorable Mention for her entry into Mindful Living Production's essay contest, from which this anthology was populated.

10

Balance

Harmony: *physical, emotional and spiritual steadiness.*

Body, Mind, Spirit

Michele J. Inge

The busy post-partum shift had begun. I started my rounds to complete each patient's vital signs before the nurses were done giving report to the next shift. The mundane activity had been done so many times, I could complete it with my eyes closed.

I entered the last patient's room at the end of the hallway. In the corner of the room was a young, thin-framed Native American woman curled up in her bed appearing comfortable and warm. She was wearing glasses too big for her face and lenses so thick they obscured her eyes.

"Hello, my name's Michele. I'm your nursing assistant today. I need to take your blood pressure, please." The woman nodded. As I wrapped the blood pressure cuff around her arm, I realized this patient had been a victim of severe physical abuse. I saw scars on her delicate arms, bald patches on her scalp, and scattered bruises on her face and neck. I tried not to gasp, concerned that I might make her uncomfortable. I told her I'd be back later to check on her. She nodded as I left the room.

"How could she have allowed that to happen to her while carrying a child?" I thought to myself in disgust. I felt compelled to go back and rescue her from the abusive relationship. After completing my work I returned to her room.

She pecked at her meal like a bird. The woman began speaking of her new little boy and how happy she and her husband were. I sat quietly listening to her. The conversation continued for awhile. She lived in Havasupai Canyon with her other three children and husband. She made no mention of the abuse she was experiencing.

When I finished caring for my other patients, I asked the charge nurse if I could spend the rest of the shift with this woman. The nurse then told me the extent of the abuse that the woman had endured. My anger turned to compassion as I heard the rest of the story.

When I came back to her room, I sat near her bed and listened to her speak about how wonderful her husband was and how much she loved him. The tension grew in the back of my neck. I couldn't believe what she was saying about him, but I kept my mouth shut and continued to listen to her.

A few years after my experience with the Native American woman, I received a letter in the mail from her.

"Dear Michele," she began, "I'm writing to let you know that the children and I have left my husband. We are living on our own now and doing very well. After speaking with you that day, I prayed a long time for guidance and was given strength to do what was best for myself and my children. Thank you for sitting with me that day and just listening."

My experience with that Native American woman was over 15 years ago and it had a profound effect on me. Not only did the experience show me the rewarding gift of helping people in the nursing profession, it also taught me the importance of balancing physical, emotional and spiritual needs.

When one experiences illness or injury, there is always an imbalance in one of these areas. As nurses, it is also easy for us to lose our balance. Here are important questions to ask yourself and your patients:

Physical health. What are you doing for yourself that is physically healthy? Are you eating healthy whole foods, or are you eating mostly processed, artificial foods? How do you feel after eating these foods? Are you exercising and able to move your body freely? How do you care for the aching or ill parts of your body? Are you giving them attention? Are you taking any herbs, vitamins or supplements? Are you taking prescribed medications? How do these make you feel?

Mental health. What do you do for yourself that is mentally healthy? Is your head busy with the constant chatter of gossip, judgments and worry? Do you do any activity that helps you be more present like meditation or deep breathing exercises? Are you active in any creative hobbies or crafts? Who do you talk to when you are upset and need to vent your feelings?

Spiritual health. What do you do for yourself that is spiritually healthy? Do you believe in a higher power? Do you love yourself unconditionally? Do you love others unconditionally? Do you take time out of your day for any spiritual rituals?

How we, as nurses, achieve physical, mental and spiritual balance impacts our wellbeing and the wellbeing of every person we touch.

Michele J. Inge, RN, MS, FNP-C

"In moments of immobilizing frustration, I make sure I take care of myself by providing myself time for the things that comfort me like yoga, meditation, drumming, and deep breaths!"

Michele Inge has recently been practicing as a Certified Family Nurse Practitioner at North Country Community Health Center, which serves mostly under-insured and state–insured patients of Northern Arizona. She has been working in the nursing profession for over 15 years, first as a Certified Nursing Assistant and then a Registered Nurse in emergency, ICU, and float pool for public healthcare settings.

Since becoming a Certified Family Nurse Practitioner, Michele has become very interested in integrative medicine and hopes to evolve her practice more in this direction. She foresees doing this by improving her skills and knowledge base in western family medicine, incorporating her abilities in Reiki Master healing, Crystal Therapy, and Shamanic journeying work, and by referring patients to alternative healthcare providers in her community.

11

Awaken

To Become Conscious: *to arouse from a sleep-like state.*

Medicine Buddha

Diana Keyes

The practice of medicine and healing have been synonymous in the Tibetan Buddhist tradition for many centuries. I began to study and practice Buddhist meditation many years ago, well before I began nursing school. In the course of practicing both nursing and Buddhism, my career path necessarily blended with the Buddhist Eightfold Path. In nearly 23 years of nursing practice, I have been employed in many areas including Neurosurgery and Trauma Intensive Care Units, the Emergency Room, Labor and Delivery, Home Health, Psychiatry and Substance Abuse, and School Nursing. The following is a "medical adaptation" of the Eightfold Path that has guided and sustained me.

I. RIGHT VIEW: Practitioners with Right View develop intuition in their area of endeavor that enables them to sense the nature and acuity of an injury. Be present to the whole individual. S/he may need assistance to cope with *how* to accept assistance and reassurance as well as pain and suffering. Healers see the *anguish* of the illness or injury. Healing anguish requires great patience and proceeds only when there is an *engagement* between the healer and the sufferer. Grasp the *nature* of the individual *before* you grasp his or her body.

II. RIGHT INTENTION: A healing practitioner overcomes personal biases, values and reactions in order to provide compassionate care. The poet, Rumi, wrote, "Out beyond the place of right-doing and wrong-doing, there is a field. I'll meet you there." Make a commitment to focus, and to *do no harm*! Patients bring to you the vulnerability inherent in their injuries or illnesses, *as well as* their dependence on your skill and care; bring your respect, along with your skills and knowledge.

III. RIGHT SPEECH: *Greet* your patient. Speak slowly and clearly *without medical jargon*, and avoid giving *too much* information. (An occasional sophisticated or well-educated individual may find it *comforting* to objectify his/her problem but let the *patient* give you that cue, and then proceed slowly.) ***Never*** *lie* but *respect the enormity of fearful anticipation*. For example, an argument is not in order for receiving a vaccination, but neither is the lie that it "won't hurt." Keep it simple: "This will hurt like being pinched hurts, *and then it will stop hurting*." *Then go ahead without bargaining.* If you feel rushed or overwhelmed by the anguish of your patient or the situation, take a deep breath *before* you enter the room. Give a genuine, kind smile, and tell your patient that you are there to help.

IV. RIGHT ACTION: Remember, "Right Patient, Right Drug, Right Dose, Right Route"? Vigilance is essential to all medical practice. Stay up-to-date in the area of your practice. Renew your skills regularly. You will be confronted with unimaginable situations that require your patience, understanding, expertise and compassion. You must be equal to the task, or *know* that you are *not*. *Healing* your patient depends on your ability to act in a non-judgmental manner as much as on your knowledge and skills.

V. RIGHT LIVELIHOOD: Aspire to become a compassionate healer. We all have "big bad nurse" stories (read Ken Kesey's, One Flew Over the Cuckoo's Nest). Find your niche and *keep on* finding it. You may (as I did) find *several*! A nurse with a wide knowledge base and superior writing skills may function well as a researcher or teacher. A nurse with a high level of calm acceptance and self-knowledge often performs well in a mental health or substance abuse treatment setting. A nurse oriented to predictability may function better in a long term care facility than in an Emergency Room. "Know thyself," William Shakespeare wrote. You will know that you have "arrived" when you feel as if you are being paid to do something you love.

VI: RIGHT EFFORT: Healing has fragile beginnings. Many patients get "repaired" but not healed; others are "healed," though their bodies may be beyond "repair." Respect the being in front of you with your undivided attention. Resist the urge to "lay on hands" immediately (emergencies excepted). Be deliberate and gentle in providing assistance and ***move slowly,*** *especially with your hands*. Though you may not wear white, the setting and your title precede you like a two inch, 12 gauge sharp! Give a running verbal account of what you are doing *in advance* of doing it, and ***move slowly***! (Don't skip this step with your unconscious and comatose patients!) When appropriate, invite patients to assist you with their care. Of course, you *know* not to give choices where none exist, but take time to *provide* creative choices as often as possible. (For example, "Do you need a minute to think this over?") A patient given choices *engages* in healing.

VII: RIGHT MINDFULNESS: Ill and injured people *need your serenity*. Practicing the healing arts places you in a position of trust. *Resist categorizing patients* by reminding yourself that each one is a *unique individual with unique needs. Know your limitations* unashamedly, so that your patients and coworkers *are free to know theirs*! If you work in a high acuity area, remember that you may lose perspective and become a "wounded healer." Make a daily opportunity to regain your balance and serenity—meditate, pray, exercise. Pay attention to what you say, what you eat and what you do outside your workplace. Healing is an *attitude*.

VIII. RIGHT CONCENTRATION: The soul of healing is focused attention. Just as important as learning the *skills* of practicing medicine, we must also learn the *attitude* of healing—one-pointed concentration. There are many methods and disciplines that develop the natural ability to concentrate elevated and sustained awareness. Meditation on the flow of breath to and from one's body is one such practice particularly suited to medical practitioners. Use the ABC acronym (Airway, Breathing, Circulation) to re*mind* you of a healing acronym: Alertness to Breathing by Concentration.

Draw on these principles as a source of *sustenance* rather than a source of self-judgment. And finally, move toward medical mindfulness in a gentle and kind manner toward your patients *and* toward yourself.

Diana Keyes, RN, ADN, BA, MALS

"Patients bring to you the vulnerability inherent in their injuries or illnesses, as well as their dependence on your skill and care; bring your respect, along with your skills and knowledge."

Diana Keyes is a practicing Buddhist, writer and nurse. She has an extensive background in psychology and education.

Diana has over 23 years of nursing experience. She has been employed in many areas including Neurosurgery and Trauma Intensive Care Units, the Emergency Room, Labor and Delivery, Home Health, Psychiatry and Substance Abuse, and School Nursing.

Along the way, Diana has received many honors and awards in the field of writing, including the Gaines Fellow in the Humanities, the Kentucky Dantzel Award for Fiction, and the Kentucky Traveling Scholars Award. Diana also contributed the winning essay in Mindful Living Production's essay contest, from which this anthology was populated.

12

Praxis

Practice: *putting into action an art, science or skill.*

Mindfulness Practice and Nursing Praxis: Keys to Wholeness

Diane Lauver

Growing up, our family attended the Methodist church every Sunday. Sometimes, I felt the beauty of silence there. Sometimes in youth group, I experienced a sense of connectedness—with myself, other, nature or the Divine. Sometimes in choir, I appreciated how music could transport us beyond where we were physically. But, the Christ story did not resonate consistently with meaning for me.

As an adult, I sought more silent practices. Figuratively and literally, the sound of the mindfulness bell brought me to my spiritual home. To me, spirituality refers to sensing meaning, feeling connected—to others, nature of the Divine—and experiencing a state beyond the 'here and now'. Although meditative mindfulness can be practiced in a secular context, for me it is a spiritual experience.

In this essay, I will share how meditative mindfulness can be spiritually sustaining for us as nurses and will offer examples of mindfulness from my personal and professional life.

To clarify, mindfulness is the practice of being fully aware of each moment. Mindfulness is about being in the present—the current moment—and being present, attentive or aware. This is the opposite of intense multi-tasking. For example, with mindfulness we focus only on the sensations of our breath, strong feelings, or birds calling. As a practice, we realize perfection is out of our reach; yet, without judgment, we begin again. With regular practice, we have opportunities to feel an emotional calm, a quiet mind, a relaxed body, and a sense of peace, richness, joy and wholeness.

Nursing, too, is a practice. We don't assume we have reached perfection; rather, we strive to improve our skills. Nursing also involves praxis—putting into action our core beliefs and values. We act not only to assist patients in managing their disease, but also to prevent disease and promote health, i.e., soundness in body, mind and spirit.

Although a busy clinical setting may not seem conducive to mindfulness, we can practice mindfulness there. A foundation of mindfulness practice is the focus on one's breath. We can take three slow, deep, even and fine breaths from our bellies, focus only on inhalation and exhalation, and let go of other thoughts, feelings and sensations. (You know, what we tell our patients to do during procedures.) We can breathe like this longer when feeling more stressed even if we have to find a bathroom to do so.

We can practice breathing briefly at chosen times in the day. Some nurses practice breathing while waiting for elevators or red-lights, or while walking down a hall. One nursing professor suggested that students take cleansing breaths as they reached for the doorknobs of their next patients' room, preparing to be present.

Repeating short breath poems (i.e., gathas) can assist our practice, to quiet over active thoughts and strong emotions. One gatha from my teacher, Thich Nhat Hahn, is "Breathing in, I calm body and mind. Breathing out, I smile. Breathing in, I know that this is the present moment. Breathing out, I know that this is the only moment." When abbreviated, this becomes "Calm,

Smile; Present moment, only moment."

If we practice mindfulness for a period each day, just 10-20 minutes, then we can drink from a spiritual well; our inner garden can blossom. One teacher said, "Just as we cannot win a race without practice, so too we are not prepared for difficulties unless we practice mindfulness when we don't need it." When I make time for morning practice, I often have calmer, richer days, a sense of flow and smoother connections with others (and my computer!)

When interacting with patients, we can listen intentionally. We can relate with an open mind, without judgment and be comfortable with silences. We can engage in deep listening as described by mindfulness teachers. We can be a "therapeutic presence" as described by nursing leaders. We can hear what is not being said.

From this space, we can speak words of support and truth. We can offer words of confidence to patients learning self-care or ask an anxious patient if he is scared of the uncertainty he faces.

When we open our hearts to patients' suffering with physical or emotional symptoms, then we engage in com-passion. ("Com"- means "with"; "pati" means "to suffer" in Latin.) As nurses, we engage in com-passion to ease our patients' suffering. Yet, with such engagement, we can also receive a gift of sacred connection. Receiving compassion—as a patient or as a caregiver—also can result in subtle healing or a major transformation. These shifts can motivate us to align our actions with our beliefs and values.

When acting with patients, we are challenged to see their multi-dimensionality. In doing so, we might see them as different from ourselves. We also can see them as similar to ourselves, in their inner goodness. If we see patients in their Wholeness, then we may understand their reluctance to follow certain medical recommendations and be tolerant of their refusal to adopt some good health behaviors. This empathy may keep us from being frustrated with the situation, and didactic or paternalistic when we propose actions.

Without cushion-time to connect within ourselves, we are less likely to listen well, speak truthfully, and act compassionately. When we do not connect meaningfully with friends, nature, or the Divine, we are more likely to experience spiritual distress. Without creating sacred space for real connections with patients, our job can lose its meaning. If we are spiritually dry, our inner garden cannot blossom and our compassion cannot flow. However, if we remain grounded in meditative mindfulness, we can feel more connected, sense meaning, and experience states beyond the here and now. If we as nurses practiced mindfulness regularly, on the cushion, street or job, then we could be refreshed and sustained by drinking at a spiritual well.

Dr. Diane Ruth Lauver

"Whether I encounter system barriers to quality patient care or interpersonal barriers to smooth collaboration, initially, I may exercise or vent with a trusted colleague to calm down. Then I sleep on the issue to avoid overreacting. The next morning I meditate and/or journal to look at my role more honestly."

Dr. Diane Lauver began her nursing career focusing on primary care issues of prevention and health promotion. In her undergraduate program, she took the credits equivalent for minors in both religion and art. However, at that time nursing students could not have official minors—perhaps because nursing students should be dedicated only to nursing? In graduate studies at the University of Rochester in New York, she obtained preparation both as a nurse practitioner and as a researcher with a focus in women's health. While in her graduate programs, she participated in a church community that was led by ministers who used inclusive language from the pulpit that was new and most welcome. These ministers engaged in critical, contextual analysis of scriptures that was refreshing.

After assuming a teaching position at University of Wisconsin-Madison School of Nursing, Diane studied women's spirituality and T'ai chi for several years. She has participated in formal Mindfulness Meditation programs, read related materials, and practiced on her own. As a nurse practitioner in women's health, Diane sees how the context of women's lives influences their health and how mind-body-spirit issues arise in primary care. As a professor, she incorporates content in mind-body-spirit practices in nurse practitioner and elective courses. Her personal practices include T'ai chi and meditative mindfulness, primarily in the tradition of Thich Nhat Hahn. She sits regularly with the Snowflower Sangha in Madison, Wisconsin where she feels she has returned home.

13

Escape

Flight From Confinement:

Distraction or relief from routine.

Eye of the Hurricane

Eddie Lueken

The trauma ICU sounds like a swarm of bees as off-going nurses whisper vital information to oncoming staff. I sip bitter coffee and review the chart of bed one. He was impaled for an unknown amount of time by a street sign after ejection from his vehicle. He will die today, as his family wishes to withdraw life support. I am here to ensure one aspect of his care—to control his pain.

I am a pain management nurse at a Level 1 trauma center. Some say I am a natural at it. I don't feel natural at anything lately, even at being a human.

"Excuse me, honey, do you think I could talk one more time to the brain doctor about my son?" Her red, swollen eyes betray a controlled panic as I detect the aqua blue color identical to the eyes in bed one. Families need reassurance before we remove the tube that keeps a body alive. I dial the number of the neuro resident and his response is predictable.

"Good God, how may times do I need to go over this with her?" He is post call, at the end of a 24 hour shift, and adds, "Can't you handle it?"

"Well, huh, let me see if someone around here can answer her questions," I say while watching her expression. The resident is incoherent with exhaustion; unable to imagine that the patient's mother is mentally listing reasons she should not kill herself when her son is gone. As I escort her to a chair and hand her a cup of coffee, I fear my good years are slipping away, lost in this vacuum of the broken-hearted. A trauma surgeon taps me on the shoulder.

"Hey, glad I ran into you. Can you figure out the methadone dose for my gunshot in room three? And follow him all next week so it doesn't get screwed up, will ya?" Well over six and a half feet tall, he exudes physical and intellectual stamina, a good quality when five twisted bodies simultaneously arrive at the trauma bay.

"I'll see him now, but I leave town tonight for a week," I reluctantly inform him. The giant surgeon grimaces, shrugs, and shuffles through the intimidating automatic steel doors and yells back, "Somebody needs to cover for you, this is ridiculous." I say nothing in response and turn back to my patient's mother.

"Oh, dear, how do you do your job?" says the numb looking woman with blue eyes.

"Just like this," I say.

Twenty-eight hours later, my husband and I, wrapped in a green army blanket, rocket across the purplish-gray bay of the Gulf of Mexico aimed at Dog Island—a seven-mile strip of sand dunes and pine trees. This bridgeless barrier island, nestled among three other islands in the Northwestern panhandle of Florida, has captivated me for over 15 years. It is raw, rugged, and best of all, cold and isolated in January.

Our hired boat captain, Dave, drives this 23-foot Aqua Sport cruiser over waves nearly my height, only to slam us down with enough force to crumble our teeth. Dave smiles warmly at us without concern that the icy wind or jolting bounces would send less hearty folk to the emergency room with frostbite and ruptured discs. I yank my ski cap over my ears and grip the seat's edge with soggy woolen mittens.

Like a scene out of Gilligan's Island, a tree-lined bank protrudes through the fog. This is the point where I start forgetting the desperate way patients look at me upon learning I am leaving town and can only be reached by cell phone in an emergency.

We dock and walk a few blocks to the Pelican Inn, the solitary hotel on Dog. There is no such thing as getting lost here. One road goes north and south, another goes east and west. With a population of 12, we see nobody and hear nothing except the crash of the temperamental Gulf.

We pass houses with names like "Blues Away," and "Gull Cottage." I think about my obsession with the old black and white movie, The Ghost and Mrs. Muir. Recently widowed, Mrs. Muir takes her daughter and maid off to live in Gull Cottage perched above the roaring surf, where she soon encounters the ghost of a sea captain, the previous owner of the house. It's a tale of love and risk-taking, punctuated with the late night sound of a lonely foghorn.

I cannot articulate why that movie and this island evoke in me the same soulful yearning. If I had to take a stab at it, I'd guess it has to do with escaping the daily routine of showing up in a hospital every day reassuring all that everything is better than it actually is.

Landing in a house like Gull Cottage, leaving behind monitor alarms and people sobbing in the ICU, who would I be? I wonder what parts of me are hidden, like the fragile reef out there, off shore, full of life and color, but well camouflaged from superficial sight. Without the numbing effects of the local martini bar and the loud roar of my colleagues pontificating on the injustices of our world, what would I have to think or say out loud? I have six days to stare at the horizon and ponder these questions. No answers are necessary.

Weeks later, a wounded, drug addict with a bloody ax tattoo, threatens to "kick my ass if I don't get rid of his pain." The stillness of a winter season on a wind swept island fills my head. He gives me the finger. I feel the thin edge of a miniature sand dollar in the pocket of my lab coat and smile. I choose this hurricane of a job and imagine the animated reef, content in its own silent existence, buried deep under the black, enraged surf.

Eddie L. Lueken, RN, BSN

"When politics and money obstruct patient care you will be the warriors that guard the bedside, keeping society focused on how civilized people should treat the ill and injured."

Eddie Leuken received a BSN in 1977. Her primary clinical experience has been in the operating room, medical-surgical, and for the last 10 years, pain management.

Eddie was awarded a grant from the *Kentucky Foundation for Women* to continue work on a collection of poetry about her career in the field of pain management.

In 2004, she was St. Joseph Hospital's "Nurse of the Year", in Phoenix, Az. She is currently enrolled in a creative non-fiction program at Phoenix College.

Eddie was awarded an Honorable Mention for her entry into Mindful Living Production's essay contest, from which this anthology was populated.

14

Teacher

Guide: *Implies intimate knowledge of the way.*

Spirituality in Nursing Education

Jane Vernon Lutz

I am a very practical person and so my approach to spirituality is also down-to-earth. I love using my spirituality to solve problems and to receive guidance and to get direction. As a psychiatric nurse, I use a spiritual approach for emotional and spiritual healing. I am spiritual when I go to the deepest aspects for myself and act from there. This feels natural and easy and results in a lovely feeling of rightness. The struggle of forcing things to happen, the mental gyrations of considering every aspect and the stress of finding a way are gone. I just flow rather effortlessly into and through situations.

We all have love at the center of our being. This is our deepest motivation as well as our deepest desire. Some aspect of love is the answer to all problems and the answer to healing in any situation. I realize that this may sound superficial and a bit simplistic, but I find the truth of it profound and deeply meaningful.

In my work with students, I find that approaching them with the most loving and accepting attitude works best for me. I am comfortable with the authority of my own personal power, which allows them to be comfortable with theirs. When I look at a student in the most positive light, I see someone who is interested in learning, someone with their own strengths and creativity and a desire for enrichment. The learning experience then progresses easily. When my expectations are positive, my outcomes are also mostly positive. If I enter into a teaching moment with a negative mindset, thinking that the students are slow or resistant or angry or any number of other negative evaluations, then reality most often follows my perception.

Problems exist in any form of practice and it is the way in which we approach the solution that illustrates the spiritual attitude. I always pray for my students. I pray that they will quickly and easily learn the material, that they will find their way in the profession and that they will find satisfaction and fulfillment in their work. I also meditate and send them positive healing energy to illuminate their paths. I look at each of them as having a bit of God within and I keep that in mind as I work with them. I respect each of them and honor their uniqueness. I ask for guidance and direction for myself and to know that my approach with each one is for our highest mutual good. I ask to know that my work is fulfilling the will of God, and I know this to be true when I have that calm feeling of rightness.

When I work with students I consciously avoid a “them and us” attitude and see us as a unit working together toward a common goal. Each is a reflection of the other. What I identify in them is also present within me. When I find that the reflections create a negative emotional response within me, then I must go into my own personal healing arsenal to free myself from the negative bonds.

While I am comfortable knowing that I have more knowledge and experience in the field than my students, I am also comfortable accepting the wisdom that students give me. Students are great teachers. We are together in the situation, each of us with valuable gifts to offer and each of us able to assist the other.

The students I work with in mental health nursing often come with issues of their own that need healing. Healing may happen consciously when we discuss and work with the problems, or they may have their concerns worked out in other ways. The healing may occur with or without my help, but it is often a major aspect of the students' learning. I meditate about students who are having difficulty and work both in the classroom and in the meditation room with them. If I am unable to work with a student on a personality level then I make the contact with his or her higher self in meditation and communicate through that avenue. I also often work on the development of the group process in clinical groups using the spiritual levels. My quest is always to help the students achieve as much knowledge, creativity and self-awareness as possible.

Love, acceptance, unity, prayer, healing and service are the aspects of spirituality that I use with students. As I practice the spiritual principles in my professional and personal life, I have developed great trust and confidence in them. They give me the assurance of knowing that I am approaching things in the very best ways that I can.

Jane Vernon Lutz, RN, MSN

"Know yourself."

Jane Lutz has always worked in some aspect of behavioral health nursing, either in practice or teaching. Her exploration of spirituality began with a meditation class, and this led her to the study of metaphysics, holistic healing methods, nature elements and ecotherapy. Jane has taught nursing, maintained a private counseling practice and developed a healing garden.

15

Service

Gives Good: *contribution to the welfare of others.*

A Call to Nursing

Dawn Marino

I was 11 years old in 1967 when I received my calling to become a nurse. That warm summer morning the sun streamed through the bedroom window illuminating the final pages of the Cherry Ames nursing novel I was finishing. I closed the cover of the book and in the sunny glow of the room my heart changed forever. There were no trumpets or visions. No booming baritones announced my fate. But there in that quiet golden moment, I began to weep for the certainty that I would be a nurse. I would care for strangers, bring them comfort and tenderly touch their lives.

A tumultuous decade intervened and it was not until 11 years later at age 22 that I began studying for my BSN. I graduated Magna Cum Laude from Arizona State University in 1982 and my journey of spiritual service through nursing began. Like most novices, I had little understanding of what I had gotten into. Oh, I knew technical skills would be required of me to accurately assess and intervene in patients' responses to trauma and illness, and like most "new grads," I was overwhelmed by the knowledge that if I had a bad day or made a mistake, someone's health or life could be at stake. What I didn't know was that each patient and family member I served would make an imprint upon my soul. That wasn't taught in nursing school.

I ministered for 10 years with my heart and hands with no

regard at all to the accumulating baggage in my spirit. I worked Med/Surg units and then moved into ER. There the intensity of human contact was ratcheted to its highest possible level. People expected my maximum attention for their cuts, burns, and bruises while in other rooms people died despite my best efforts as part of their health care team. My soul was stamped with human suffering 12 hours a day, three days a week.

It took a long while for me to notice the heaviness that was building within me. Then a patient injured me while I was helping save her life from an intentional overdose. I snapped. I was filled with anger. I felt I had no compassion left.

This was burnout and I knew it. I transferred to Labor and Delivery in hopes it would renew my commitment to compassionate care. After all, what could be better than bringing new life into the world? Many births indeed inspired me. Some sucked me drier than ER ever could. Unprepared mothers agonized by labor pleaded with me as though I alone could ease their suffering. Families expected high tech births with no pain or risk and blamed me if either expectation was not met. Babies died or were injured by the arduous journey through the birth canal. My soul collected more imprints. I returned with little enthusiasm to ER.

Are you wondering at this stage in the narrative what happened to the 11-year-old girl's belief in nursing? It was still in me. Despite my spiritual distress, I never lost sight of my love of caring for others. I felt I was a natural healer. My peers and patients had told me as much, so what could I do?

I had a particularly grueling shift one night. A beautiful seven-year-old girl died due to carbon monoxide poisoning in the back of her parent's pickup. The mother sobbed in my arms. Nothing I did could remove her pain from my heart. I had to try something new. I sat in prayer and asked Spirit how I was to continue in nursing. This was my question, "What does it mean to be a healer in this place?" It was 1992. I was 36.

Shortly thereafter I discovered the American Holistic Nurses Association. I attended a conference they sponsored with Barbara Dossey, RN, Ph.D. The topic was Caring for the Caregiver. I credit the techniques Dr. Dossey taught that day with initiating my understanding of spiritual sanity in nursing.

I began to use breathing and visualization to surround myself with white light before every shift and during the shift when I needed a boost. I noticed immediately I wasn't as tired when my 12-hour shift was done. Soon I began using my commute time as prayer time asking that I be filled with divine guidance just to help me get through the day. It didn't take long before I had enough spare energy to also pray that I be guided helping patients in a way they might best accept and understand. I felt a new lease on my career as spiritual servant through nursing. In no time, I was even able to offer prayers of thanks for the opportunity to serve.

My career path has evolved over the past 13 years. I have studied and taught many holistic nursing techniques and philosophies. I now work holistically in private practice and in a Cardiopulmonary Rehabilitation setting. All this is a tribute to what can happen when a simple question is asked. My path to understanding what it is to be a healer in this place is an adventurous journey. I have elaborated my prayers for guidance and my visualizations of protection. I have learned to remember my connection to the Earth and the sustenance it gives me under any circumstance. I have come to value the support and camaraderie of other nurses with similar patient care values. Most importantly, I remind myself often of the value of this moment—the present—where human interaction can heal both patient and caregiver.

My mother always told me, "you cannot pour from an empty cup." My journey in nursing as a spiritual practice has shown me the truth of this. I will devote the rest of my career to filling my spiritual cup so that it can run abundantly over and fill the cups of those I serve.

Dawn E. U. Marino, RN, BSN, HNC

"What I am most grateful for in my nursing experience is that it has stretched my soul beyond anything I could have imagined as a young woman and forced me to birth my own self transformation through the fire of caring so deeply and intimately for others."

Dawn Marino graduated Magna cum Laude in 1982 from Arizona State University with a BSN. Her nursing career includes two years in medical/surgical nursing, 10 years in emergency nursing, and 14 years practicing holistic nursing. Since 1992 Dawn has accumulated certifications in holistic healthcare, which include Biofeedback, Healing Touch, Holistic Nursing, and Clinical Aromatherapy. She is a trained HealthRhythms drum circle facilitator and a licensed FitRhythms instructor. Dawn practices and teaches holistic health and healing in her private practice and at Navapache Regional Medical Center. Dawn established the hospital's Integrative Health Care Department. She uses a holistic approach with patients in the Cardiac Rehabilitation program, and with Emergency Department staff employing biofeedback for stress reduction. Her private practice includes individual healing/coaching sessions and drum circles for therapeutics and fitness.

Dawn was awarded an Honorable Mention for her entry into Mindful Living Production's essay contest, from which this anthology was populated.

16

Asklepios

Olympian God: *the only god who remained close to suffering man.*

The Spiral of Healing: Ancient Healing and Modern Medicine

Loretta D. Melancon

The trip to Greece was just my style—organized and structured with tours planned so that we'd accomplish as much as possible in a short period of time. This proved to be a detriment near the end of my second day when the tour bus stopped at the town of Epidaurus. The tour guide had given us a brief history of the archaeological site of the sanctuary of Asklepios, the god of medicine. After visiting the theater as a group, we were advised that we had 20 minutes to explore the site and museum before boarding the bus for the return trip to Athens. With so little time I made a hurried pass through the museum then headed out into the ruins alone to find the site of the temple and Abato, the building where pilgrims spent the night anticipating a message from a god and a cure for their illness. All I wanted to do was stand on that sacred spot and experience it as best I could these 2000 years later. You can imagine my frustration when the 20 minutes elapsed and I felt completely lost among the foundations of so many unrecognizable buildings. I managed to calm myself and collect my thoughts as I realized that I had a choice about how I would experience this dilemma and opted to make the best of it by sitting quietly among the ruins, closing my eyes, and asking to be able to take away with me an image of my inner healer.

Throughout the first centuries of the sanctuary's existence, the written sources never mention medical intervention by the priests. Healing occurred solely with the appearance of the god Asklepios and was attributed to Him alone. However, over the centuries as medicine developed, faith in divine intervention was shaken and the sanctuary at Epidaurus was faced with the likelihood of losing its patrons. The priesthood was therefore obliged to modernize and began to intervene in the treatment by assessing pilgrims' ailments and giving primary instructions. The pilgrims, now more fittingly called patients, continued to spend the night in the Abato and Asklepios appeared as before. In the morning patients related their dreams to the priests who, using their medical knowledge, interpreted the god's instructions and prescribed the therapeutic interventions accordingly. Of course, the patients were advised to remain within the sanctuary for the prescribed treatment. Thus, the sanctuary developed into a hospital while remaining a religious center.

The temple continued to expand into a social center with hot and cold baths, guest houses, gymnasia, contests, and theatrical performances all available in a serene and pleasant environment. This progressive stance allowed the sanctuary to achieve a second acme in the second century C.E. Even when the belief in the Olympian gods wavered when faced with the general triumph of Christianity, Asklepios was the only god who remained close to suffering man. As late as the fourth century C.E., pilgrims still slept in the Abato in the hope of a cure. Only during enemy incursions in C.E. 395 was the sanctuary destroyed, and the gates permanently closed by 426. Two great earthquakes in the sixth century completed the destruction and reduced the magnificent buildings to ruins that weren't excavated until 1861.

It was among these ruins that, while the tour bus waited, I sought out my own inner healer and was surprised and intrigued by what seemed to be a dream. Almost immediately a nautilus shell appeared. Although this image had no significance for me,

I was out of time and had no choice but to leave Epidarus with this unexpected symbol, trusting that the meaning would eventually become clear to me.

The nautilus is a mollusk of the Pacific and Indian Oceans that has not changed in 450 million years and is indeed a living fossil. Its growth begins with crisis. When the walls of its world seem to be narrowing down, creating a "crunch" and hemming the animal in, it is forced to create a new space, pushing beyond the old boundaries by secreting a new, larger chamber and walling off the one left behind. The nautilus uses its outgrown chambers (its past, you might say) to maintain its balance and facilitate movement in the present. Although the nautilus carries the unique story of its past wherever it goes, the past does not weigh it down. Instead, age and maturity actually enhance its balance and buoyancy.

Like the maturing nautilus, we all have the potential for growing beyond what appear to be our limits. If we remain aware of the connection between past and present by choosing to access the wisdom of past experience, we too can achieve the balance and buoyancy that promote health. I often reflect on how modern healthcare has missed possibilities for growth and ignored its potential because it has become hemmed in by worn-out images of health and disease. Might modern physicians once more become true to their role as priestly guides? Might I as a nurse have creative potential just waiting to unfold in my practice?

Carl Jung reminds us "all the greatest and most important problems of life are fundamentally insolvable. They can never be solved, only outgrown. The nautilus shows us that discovery and growth involve continual crisis with moments of comfort scattered in between. In pushing past what seems to be the outer limit, new doors open, and the promise of the future unfolds. As I push past the apparent limits in my nursing practice and set my intention to become the fullness of my potential as an individual, my practice becomes *who I am*, not what I do.

May the message of the nautilus shell encourage us all to reflect on the past, live in the moment, and find hope for the future!

Loretta D. Melancon, RN, HNC

"It is more who you are as a person, in relationship with the patient, than what you do as a nurse that has the greatest impact on the overall healing process."

Loretta was born and raised in Louisiana where she received a Bachelor of Science in Nursing from the University of Louisiana at Lafayette. Before moving to California in 1997, she worked in a community hospital where she had experience in oncology nursing and also helped to coordinate a Healing Health Care Symposium while serving as Healing Health Care Coordinator at Lafayette General Medical Center. She is certified in holistic nursing through the American Holistic Nurses' Certification Corporation, has organized local holistic nursing networks, and offers workshops to introduce other nurses to holistic principles. Additional teaching experience includes several classes offered through Santa Barbara City College's Continuing Education Division as well as teaching CPR as a Basic Life Support instructor for the American Heart Association. In addition, she represents other holistic educators by coordinating workshops and speaking engagements that advocate for integrating holistic healing principles and practices with allopathic medicine. She is presently residing in Hot Springs Village, Arkansas where she is an avid hiker and has assumed a leadership position with Friends of the Ouachita

Trail, a non-profit organization dedicated to preserving and maintaining the Ouachita National Recreation Trail as a healthy and enjoyable outdoor recreational asset.

The intention of her work in the varied forms it takes is always, first, to guide patients to resources that can create healing environments – physically, mentally, emotionally and spiritually – which provide the “conditions” needed by Nature to act on their behalf.

Loretta was awarded an Honorable Mention for her entry into Mindful Living Production’s essay contest, from which this anthology was populated.

17

Intention

Manifestation: *having the mind, attention, or will concentrated on creating some end or purpose.*

Concious Intention Toward a More Peaceful Life

Doris Popovich

Growing up, I attended a small Methodist church, and both my parents were active in church leadership. There, I learned the complex nature of a spiritual community. I also learned that I could see, hear, and touch God when I got quiet. By the time I reached confirmation age, I had abandoned the notion that only Christians "made it to heaven." I believed intuitively that there were many paths to many gods. This belief continues to be the heart-center of my spiritual exploration. I am a spiritual being having a human experience with unlimited opportunities to express my divine nature. I believe this is true for all of us.

God is everywhere—in all things. All physical matter, including our bodies, is composed of the same recycled material: carbon, hydrogen, oxygen, nitrogen and small amounts of other elements. What distinguishes one energy mass from another is its vibration. Higher density matter, like trees and tables, has microscopically faster vibrations than our bodies, or our thoughts. But our bodies and our thoughts also create measurable energy. Even though we may feel separate from a tree or a flower or a coworker, in fact, we are all a part of the same vibrating mass. This is not a supposition but rather a mathematical certainty celebrated within the field of Quantum Mechanics. The major difference between a human being and a table is that we have a nervous system capable of awareness of our energy and intellect capable of directing information to transform our energy.

There are no well-defined edges in Quantum Mechanics; there are only localized variations. In effect, the universe, and all it holds, is our extended body. What separates us from all other life on this planet is our ability to set conscious intentions. Our intentions are powerful attractors of outcome. We've all heard the expression "Be careful what you wish for." Thanks to Quantum Mechanics, we now know why this is true.

Thoughts held in mind are outpictured in experience. Imagine this, our thoughts—what we think about all day, those quiet unspoken moments of internal dialogue—are actually the blueprints for today's experience. According to physicists specializing in Quantum Mechanics, we are always attracting and exchanging energy, and this energy organizes itself according to our thoughts and feelings, thereby creating our reality. We turn out to be far more powerful participants in how our lives unfold than most of us like to admit.

According to this science, thoughts held in mind attract like energy to affect changes in our lives and in our world. This is the power of conscious intention. To say that one person can't make a difference is mathematically impossible! So I ask myself, what kind of difference am I making today?

In the end, I believe the most beneficial, loving action we can take for our profession, and for our world, is to find personal peace. Marianne Williamson said it best in the introduction to her spiritual masterpiece, *Everyday Grace:* "For as any one of us finds our wings, the entire world is lifted."

Change your thinking, change your life. Sounds simple enough—if you live in a cave. But there are no caves in nursing. You are "out there" every minute, dealing with human suffering, dealing with the state of madness brought about by financial pressures to practice the art of healing faster.

In my morning meditation I practice remembering that I am a

powerful spiritual expression and that my conscious intentions directly create my experience and my world. I'm not implying or suggesting that I ever fully achieve these conscious intentions. There are days though when I retire my ego and succeed at "getting out of the way." On those days I feel immensely peaceful. Here are a few of the specific conscious intentions I work with in my daily practice toward greater peace.

* * *

Divine Love within me opens my heart to a higher expression of unconditional love and calls forth my joyful, fearless millionaire. I used to think that money and God were opposites. Now I know that money is just one more form of spiritual currency with which I can change the world for good. Over time I have found that when I lovingly express my gifts and follow my passion, money flows more freely into and out of my life.

Surrender all resentments to a Higher Power. Holding onto resentments toward another person or institution is like taking poison and hoping that the other person will die. Holding onto resentments or disappointments toward myself is like taking poison. Sometimes, when I am hooked by a power struggle, I ask myself, "Would you rather be right, or happy?" Then I take a deep breath of surrender.

Give away that which you most desire. This is a Buddhist slogan that I first heard on Pema Chodron's taped series entitled, "When Everything Falls Apart". Pema Chodron is an American Buddhist nun, and a world-renowned spiritual teacher.

When I am feeling dissatisfied, I sit in meditation with this question: What is it that I most desire from this person or situation? For example, I may be feeling dissatisfied at work because I feel unheard, or disrespected, or generally unappreciated. So, I pray for the willingness to hear, respect, and appreciate my coworkers and/or my boss. Practiced over time, the situation always improves if I am truly where God means for me to be.

Abandon any hope of fruition. This is another Buddhist slogan that helps me very much. Attachment to outcome is a huge trap for me. When I surrender to the constant change around me, I am free to live moment by moment—to appreciate "what is." Knowing, really knowing, that nothing is ever going to settle down, frees me to make changes and take risks. This sounds simple, but it's not easy. Over time, I am gradually giving up the fantasy that one day—if I work really hard—everything in my life will be perfect. I am becoming more like the wind, free to explore new directions.

Divine Love within me expresses as Gratitude for every result. Without a doubt, gratitude is the cornerstone of my spiritual fitness. Granted, there are times when I do not understand the great mystery of God's plan, times when I get stuck in the grand theodicy of it all—asking why bad things happen to good people—but over time, by practicing gratitude, my sadness for the world's suffering has been replaced by hope and action. When I am challenged to enrich my spiritual life with more joy, I start where I am—with gratitude for *every* result!

Doris J Popovich, RN, MA
Principal, Touch of Eden Garden Design

"In the end, I believe the most beneficial, loving action we can take for our profession, and for our world, is to find personal peace."

Doris describes herself as a nurse, writer and entrepreneur – in equal measure.

She has worked for 26 years as a Behavioral Health Nurse, in every possible capacity and setting. Currently she works part-time for Resurrection Home Health Services, in Chicago.

She is a published author, with numerous poems, short stories, and creative nonfiction pieces in print. She has performed her work many times in many venues. She loves a captive audience!

Doris also shares ownership of a booming garden design business, called Touch of Eden. She and Mary, her domestic partner of 20 years, founded this company five years ago. One day they hope to retire out west where they can garden all year long!

18

Conduit

Channel: *a natural path through which something is conveyed.*

Nursing as a Spiritual Path

Patrice Rancour

I find it impossible to be a nurse and *not* be a spiritual seeker. Nurses are in one of the very few professions that are given societal sanction to lay hands on people during the most intimate moments of their lives, whether it be at birth, in sickness, in health, or at death. These transitions are archetypically the portals of entry into the sacred mysteries of life. It is an error in judgment to believe one will not be touched by participating in them. And often the wounds with which I most often come into contact resonate with my own, so that healing is possible for all, myself included. This is the archetype of the wounded healer, and it makes it possible for my work to be the vehicle for my own healing. As such, I find, much as Marsha Sinetar writes that "my work has become my prayer."

Work as prayer means understanding I am in "the zone" when I can move in close to someone and simultaneously let go. This means that I immerse myself fully in the present moment with the individual I am serving. It is the only thing I can control—to formalize a consciously-caring intent to be really present with that individual in the moment. This ability to be fully present is what helps us transcend the mundane and moves us into peak experiences of the eternal. Accordingly, Ram Dass instructs that the best way to prepare for the future is to be here now.

As I move in close, I am also detaching from any sense that

I can control the outcome, something over which I have no control. Praying for someone's highest good is different from praying for that individual's cure, as I have no idea whether being cured is really in that person's highest good. Detaching from the illusion that I am omniscient and omnipotent is very freeing spiritually. As the Buddhists note, it is easy to keep one's heart open in heaven but so much harder to do so in hell. When people allow me entrée into their personal hells, this detachment, this letting go, is what keeps me spiritually sane, present, able to accurately discern what is needed, and then to be able to regulate the through-flow of energy accordingly, whether it be physically, mentally, emotionally and/or spiritually. In this respect, the energy that flows through me is filling me as well as the person it is intended for.

This is most evident to me when I am providing therapies such as psychotherapy, guided imagery, massage or Reiki to people. In fact, the days I do not provide these therapies, I always feel less "full." To understand, as Helen Keller did, that although the world is full of suffering, it is also full of the overcoming of it, means that I am not sapping my own energies to give to others; rather, I see myself as part of an interconnected web, a flowing river of energy, information and consciousness, through which I can focus such efforts towards the healing of another. This permits me to give from abundance, from grace if you will, and not from emptiness. Once again, healing a life, rather than curing a body, is the goal. The first is always possible, the second not always so. It is such a relief to know that I am not responsible for someone else's healing, that I am merely a conduit whereby that person can make his or her own choices, be the choices conscious or otherwise.

I also adhere to the notion espoused by Jennifer James, Ph.D. that I am doing this work for myself, and not for others, and that I have chosen service as a means to reach a deeper understanding of self and life. This is why I find my work humbling and not depressing: others, in allowing me to be a witness to the crossroads of their lives, offer me instruction on how to live consciously and to die consciously. What a unique educational opportunity! Where else can one work in order to be so schooled? The realization that I am doing this for myself is liberating. It just so happens that the work provides that others benefit from it as well. I believe we are all hot-wired to give, and that burnout occurs due to a lack of caring, and not from caring too much.

And so, in order to make sure that work is marked by peak experiences rather than bleak ones, I believe it is necessary to develop a personal philosophy or cosmology that transcends culture, religion, schools of thought, models and such. The paths to truth are many. When asked once what his religion was, the Dalai Lama replied “human kindness.” When one can work from the meta level of compassion, rather than from micro levels of specific dogmas, rituals or theories, it becomes easier to float above what can frequently become encumbrances and meet people directly. Having access to these vehicles is merely an avenue to reach people; they are not ends in and of themselves.

And this is why I believe it is impossible for me to be a nurse and *not* be a spiritual seeker.

Patrice Rancour, RN, MS, CS

"With regards to my nursing profession, I am most grateful for two things: the immersion in the intimate richness of life and death experiences shared with others, and its great variety of roles and settings."

Patrice Rancour is a mental health clinical nurse specialist, and has been a practicing nurse for almost 33 years. She has worked as a clinician, educator, consultant, and most recently in health care program, policy and research. Her interests include psychoneuroimmunology, complementary and alternative therapies, and working with people who are facing life-threatening illnesses. Patrice has given numerous presentations and is published in her field.

19

Surrender

To Give Back Power: *to give one's self up.*

Mary Lu chose to die on the eve of the Epiphany. As a fledgling hospice nurse, after a career as a nurse educator and as a nurse entrepreneur, I watched my very first hospice patient embrace her impending death with unfaltering dignity.

I met Mary Lu and Bill on December 12, 2001. That was the day the couple accepted palliative or comfort care under the auspices of hospice. During the admission interview Mary Lu, age 73, dressed in a flowery chintz housecoat and satin bedroom slippers, sat at her Queen Ann dining room table sipping coffee. She smelled freshly bathed and dusted with Lilies of the Valley talc. Her fragrance blended with the aroma of the French Roast coffee she sipped. She gestured for me to fill my cup and take the chair directly across from her. Her clear blue eyes invited me in.

Alert and interested, Mary Lu listened to my explanation of hospice benefits. As her case manager, I would schedule visits several times a week and come at other times when she and her husband needed me. When I was off duty another hospice nurse would be on call. I ordered medications, a hospital bed and equipment to be delivered that afternoon. I explained hospice services, which includes visits from a social worker and a chaplain; a nursing assistant would come every third day for bath, back massage and a change of bed linens.

I began her head-to-toe physical assessment. I listened to her chest, counting the thumping under her rib cage. Her words suddenly interrupted my concentration. "According to my doctors' calculations I have one month to live." There was an involuntary jolt of my head that yanked the stethoscope from my ears. Gathering my composure I asked, "How do you feel knowing that you have one month to live?"

Her eyes lit up and widened. She gazed into the distance and serenely replied, "I am really looking forward to the journey!" I felt my face flush and the pulse in my neck pound. How could she be so open, so unafraid?

Mary Lu was my hospice patient for four and a half weeks. With each visit her energy diminished and she became bed bound. Her appetite even for soup and sherbet waned and she pushed away the hand that offered her sips of water. Tiny amounts of crushed ice that were spooned into her mouth dribbled down her chin. No longer wanting food or fluid, her body was shutting down. Her hands and feet became cool to touch and parts of her body that rested on the bed showed a purplish discoloration. These were the signs that her circulatory system was failing. Her breathing became uneven; sometimes it stopped for a few seconds and at other times became very rapid.

Even as she declined Mary Lu purred when I positioned a towel and poured lavender oil to massage her feet. With the oil I used a light pressure molding my hands to fit the contour of each foot. I attended to each toe with a gentle squeeze. The flesh of my thumbs found key pressure points on the top and bottom of her feet. Gentle smooth stroking relaxed her entire body. The music of Pachelbel's Canon in D played softly in the background.

It was my joy to pamper Mary Lu, a woman who together with her husband raised four children and taught hundreds of third graders during her 30-year teaching career.

A mini Christmas choir from hospice visited their home the evening of December 23rd. Mary Lu, wrapped in a pink down feather quilt looked like a baby doll tucked in for the night. Her eyes were closed. Her soft smile told us she enjoyed our carols. As we completed our last song she raised her arms out from under the quilt and joined her hands in a prayer gesture. No words needed. Misty-eyed and full-hearted our group of five said goodbye and walked out into the chilly December night.

Friday was my last visit. I increased the dosage of medication to lighten the restlessness that had begun. She remained alert but said nothing until I asked her the question: "Have you said all your good-byes?"

"Oh yes," she whispered, "and I am not afraid to go!" Her husband and children surrounded her bed, held her hand, stroked her hair and patted her arms. One by one, "I love you, Mom; I am sorry, Mom; we'll miss you, Mom." Then Mary Lu took a breath, gave a sigh and was gone from our sight.

Sarah Seybold, RN, MSN

"Practice attention and intention, maintain a spiritual practice, and operate from what Zen Buddhists call "beginner's mind".

After graduation from Mercy College of Nursing in San Diego, Sarah served as a Peace Corp volunteer in Turkey. She returned to complete her B.S. at University of San Francisco, and following a second Peace Corps stint on Brazil's Amazon River, earned her earned her master's at The University of California Medical Center in San Francisco.

After sixteen years of teaching in Bay Area nursing schools, she co-founded the Center of US–USSR Initiatives, which promoted understanding and harmony between the peoples of the United States and the Soviet Union. She made fourteen journeys to Russia. She became a nurse entrepreneur by establishing Dove Professional Apparel, a leading manufacturer of medical apparel.

Sarah has earned her certificate in Swedish massage, spiritual direction, and end-of-life counseling. She is also a volunteer parish nurse at Trinity Episcopal Church. She currently teaches mental health nursing at the Oregon Health Sciences University campus in Ashland.

20

Renewal

Restore: *to make new spiritually.*

Everything Happens for a Reason

Teresa Shuff

Dedicated to the compassionate care of others, nurses often neglect their own personal needs. By their very nature nurses are giving of themselves, even in their personal lives. It is not uncommon for nurses to place work, patients, children, spouses, household chores, or community needs ahead of their own. For this reason, nurses frequently experience a syndrome referred to as burn out and are unable to tap into the joys of life.

After a decade of working in the high stress environment of the Operating Rooms, I too experienced the burn out so typical in the profession. The physical signs of adrenal exhaustion such as steady weight gain, cold feet, and unrelenting fatigue were undeniable. The insidious ravages of self-neglect on mind and spirit were more difficult to detect. While taking a correspondence course on alternative and complementary therapies, I made a conscious decision to do something about my health. I consulted a chiropractor that was also trained as a naturopath. His recommendations included participation in a Mindful Based Stress Reduction Class (MBSR) and improved nutrition. Working rotating shifts, I didn't see how I could attend an eight-week MBSR class. I chose instead to focus on nutrition. I attended weekend workshops to learn how to shop for and cook with natural, whole foods.

I was well on the road to improving my body through nutrition when I stumbled onto the path of emotional and spiritual recovery quite by accident. When my uncle received a heart transplant, family members were circulating a book that put forth the idea that the soul resides in the heart. As an OR nurse who had participated in many heart transplants, I found the book intriguing. I openly discussed the book with a co-worker and found she was already familiar with it. She, in turn, suggested other books that she thought I might find interesting. One book led to another and soon I found myself engrossed in such topics as reincarnation, karma, and collective consciousness. Through my reading I learned of a man commonly referred to as the "Sleeping Prophet": Edgar Cayce. I joined the organization he founded, the Association of Research and Enlightenment (A.R.E.), as a means of continually stoking the spiritual fires.

I was finally nurturing myself body, mind, and spirit. I felt like my old self again. Then, in January 2001, I had the wind blown out of my sails when I sustained an occupational HIV exposure from a needle stick. Within an hour of the exposure I was started on a prophylactic treatment that consisted of the same pharmaceutical cocktail taken by patients with HIV. Despite the improvement in my health to that point, the medications wreaked havoc on my body. After long days at work I would return home so sick and tired that I could do little more than lie down and watch the fish swimming in their aquarium. Towards the end of the month-long treatment I was too incapacitated to continue working. Through it all, what helped me emotionally was my newfound belief that everything happens for a reason.

As with all things, time truly does heal all wounds. As time passed and my subsequent HIV testing came back negative, I moved on with my life, once again trying to rebuild my health. When my Nurse Manager left her position I took the role she vacated. In my new role I faced new challenges, responsibilities, and stressors, but I refused to allow this to impact my spiritual quest. I now firmly believe that in my role as Nurse Manager, one of my missions is to cultivate a culture of work/life balance among the next generation of nurses, helping them to avoid the pitfalls of burn out.

Our hospital has a formal wellness program that has much to offer staff. I am a Wellness Ambassador for the program, helping staff to become aware of the resources available to them. I try to serve as a role model for healthy lifestyle habits and I'm finally participating in the Mindful Based Stress Reduction class offered through that program. In addition, I have made my many books on health and wellness, positive attitude, and spirituality available to the staff to borrow through an informal lending library. I also share the following magazines at work: Eating Well, Spirituality & Health, Body & Soul, Venture Inward, and Angels on Earth. I often copy and distribute inspirational pieces to the staff. My main source of spiritual sanity is my involvement with the A.R.E. I am very open with the staff, sharing my beliefs and personal experiences freely. Without a doubt this wellness coaching is the most rewarding aspect of my job.

One topic that staff has really been intrigued by is that of dreamwork. After I attended a workshop on dream interpretation, they were full of questions. They are aware that I seek guidance from my dreams and as a result of such guidance I am undergoing acupuncture treatments for a frozen shoulder. I recently helped a staff member interpret a dream that she thought was bizarre. In interpreting the universal symbolism I suggested that her life might be changing in such ways that it would never again be the same. I told her it was up to her to decipher the personal symbolism to figure out what that change might be. The next workday she came to me and confessed that she nearly fell over when she heard my interpretation, as she was pregnant. This opened the gates of communication regarding healthy habits for pregnancy and how to incorporate them into the work environment.

It is imperative that we, as nurses, support and encourage

each other to care for ourselves. We must dispel the idea that self-care is indulgent and selfish. One way to accomplish this is to share what practices we find helpful in our own lives. We must give ourselves permission to seek personal renewal. After all, if we are not well cared for ourselves, how can we expect to have anything of value to offer to others?

Teresa A Shuff, RN, BSN

"The advice I give all younger nurses is to live a life of balance."

Teresa Shuff went into the profession of nursing as a result of a complicated pregnancy. She graduated with a BSN in 1989 and went into the arena of Peri Operative Nursing. She started out in Adult General Surgery and Neurosurgery, and transferred into Cardiothoracic Surgery after a couple years. Teresa has been a Nurse Manager in the OR for the past several years. She is a member of the Association of Research and Enlightenment and a student of Atlantic University pursuing a Masters in Transpersonal Studies.

Teresa was awarded an Honorable Mention for her entry into Mindful Living Production's essay contest, from which this anthology was populated.

21

Brahmaviharas [Hindu]

Divine Abodes: Friendliness, compassion, sympathetic joy, and equanimity—calm wholesome qualities of a mind at rest.

"Nurse. . .!"

Jo Marie Thompson

In the current nursing milieu of our troubled, market-driven healthcare system, the notion of spiritual fitness implies less about preparedness for the service of a vocation, as it once may have, and more about keeping the faith on the field of battle, a field teeming with all the treacherous contradictions and impossible demands of any battlefield. One looks for elusive meaning in the machinery of modern healthcare, and the heart searches for an escape from seemingly inevitable compassion fatigue. There is the well known story of the elderly Zen master who, when asked "What are the fruits of a lifetime of spiritual practice?" replied, "An appropriate response." Having recently, and with some resolution, taken leave of a role I theoretically love, that of nurse and caregiver, I still can't fully put it down. Not only because I imagine economic necessity might impel future forays back into the field, but because I still hope for a truce, however uneasy, with this rude calling. I hope for an appropriate response. My response (in progress) must necessarily be rooted in Buddhism (my own background), but I think it may generalize to most heartfelt and discerning spiritual practices.

A friend once commented that a repressive government is especially unable to tolerate genuine spiritual practice in its midst because this represents an endeavor to see unflinchingly into the reality of things, and what could be more subversive than that? Sub – versive: Turning under. Seeing under. It takes this sort of eye to plumb the depths of mind and experience. Frankly, modern day healthcare can not tolerate this gaze either, which exposes greed, salesmanship, and lust for power where we are told to find benevolence and care for sentient beings. It sees delusion where we are told to believe in the futile but profitable war against mortality. It sees negligence and exacerbation of suffering where we're told to see the best medical system money can buy.

Because of this 'turning under,' the appropriate response I imagine must include a large dose of truth telling, and some measure of guerilla tactics: spiritual fitness for nursing practice in these times includes a consciousness of social justice issues and a willingness to engage this arena. The opportunities for this engagement are numerous and varied, and we must use our triage skills to determine where, how, and how much to engage, but I believe working and surviving by this system can not begin to approach honest and right livelihood without the capacity to truthfully, humbly, and pragmatically work to also mitigate the rampant harm currently underway at the hands of this same system. Whether we lobby Congress; support our labor unions; organize in professional and advocacy groups; serve underserved populations; or make the truth of the current system's enormous foibles audible by putting our voices out there, some ongoing action is crucial to our spiritual and ethical well-being.

Our best discernment and understanding of the modes of nursing available and the exercising of wise choice are crucial as well, lest we risk turning vocation into prostitution. It's no surprise that the area of nursing (and medicine) which undisputedly delivers the most effective and far reaching health and quality-of-life benefits is also the lowest paid: public health. Choosing a position based on benefit to sentient life rather than size of paycheck can be a significant sacrifice, but it's no longer one that many of us have the ease to turn away from.

Likewise, choosing professional settings which respect the health of our (staff, patients, families) minds and awareness is now an imperative as well. Institutions which promote sensory overload, abusive power dynamics, and overwhelming work loads are no longer an option for those prioritizing spiritual well being. In Buddhist training systems, restraint of the sense doors, living plainly and simply, are early requisites of the "gradual training." When awareness can be quieted and calmed, even when going about work in the world, we retain the most optimal condition for an awakening mind. A mind-heart that is awakening is a mind-heart cultivating the virtues often called for in the vocation of nursing. Called the Brahmaviharas or "divine abodes," they include friendliness, compassion, sympathetic joy, and equanimity. These are not sentimental qualities (their sentimental counterparts are known as the 'near enemies' of the Brahmaviharas and include endearment, pity, exuberance, and indifference). The Brahmaviharas are calm, wholesome qualities of a mind at rest, and for many of us can be difficult to cultivate in the common nursing environment of sensory assault. Though nursing environments more conducive to spiritual well being are rare, they do exist. If we are unable to find them, I count the decision to leave the profession as an equally appropriate response. For some of us, this restraint of the sense doors can also mean choosing to simplify our economic needs to such an extent that full-time nursing is not a necessity. I learned early on that more than three days a week of nursing was more damaging than profitable.

A lecturer in the early part of nursing school spoke so simply and believably about her camaraderie with her profession: "I feel so proud of nursing and nurses! I wouldn't do anything or be anywhere else." Her voice is still vivid to me and I feel lucky that she lodged herself so securely in my memory that now, in my best moments, I remember that I, too, am this proud of nursing. Nurses have represented the wisest, smartest, brassiest, funniest, and most capable women and men I've known. The truth is, I still want to be counted as one of them. When the Buddha was asked if a good friend wasn't half of the spiritual life, he replied: "Don't say that, a good friend is *all* of the spiritual life." His definition of a good friend was, again, not sentimental, but includes wisdom and a willingness to see clearly and awaken alongside us. May we all endeavor to befriend each other in this way, lending one another our eyes, courage, wisdom, and stamina to cultivate an appropriate response which may quietly (or not so quietly) challenge the current unholy circumstances of this daunting field of practice.

Jo Marie Thompson, RN, MN

"I am most grateful for the contact with such a diversity of people as they face extremes of life – thereby learning how to face them myself; seeing that life does *work it's magic on the human heart, sometimes by brutal methods, but by close contact with the underbelly of things, becoming a bit more 'chewed up', a bit more 'cooked' myself on the way to a tender heart."*

Jo Marie Thompson is a nursing lifer, mostly due to her belief that "once a nurse, always a nurse." She graduated in 1994 from the University of Washington with a BSN and a Palliative Care focus. She's served as a hospice nurse in Seattle, Chicago, California, and rural New Mexico, interrupted by a three-year stint in neuro-trauma in Seattle. In 2004, she earned an MN & certification in neuroscience nursing. She still considers Hospice to be her true nursing calling. Her strategy to survive nursing as a lifer is to take frequent long breaks, maintain a strong spiritual practice, and concurrently pursue alternate life work. She currently resides and works full time at a small Buddhist center in Illinois. Her favorite teacher describes spiritual awakening as a "public health measure," so she believes this work still qualifies her as a nurse. She is unsure what her next "official" nursing endeavor will be.

Observe and You Will Know

Observe a forgotten down feather wind-dancing
Above and across an alpine forest
And you will know me.

I am mist of rain nurturing a fern crosier
With elements carbon and spirit through
Reed-beds thick as wool.

I am day Light and breath coercing a lily
To bloom in a pond so lifeless even
The gnats don't bother.

I am the warm belly of a February
Goose staring down midnight winds to daybreak
Knowing seasons pass.

I am Love chiseling through midsternal heart ice
In seasons of awakening when our
Eyes finally meet.

~ Doris J. Popovich

Looking for the Perfect Gift for the Nurses in Your Life?

21 Peaceful Nurses is guaranteed to be a source of hope and inspiration, a way of honoring the spiritual paths of nurses practicing peace in the workplace.

Quantity	Discount	Your Cost
1		$14.95
2-9	10%	$13.45
10-99	15%	$12.70
99+	Call (877) 235-4515 for rates	

All books delightfully autographed upon request!

Subtotal	$
Illinois Sales Tax, (IL res only) (@ .875)	$
Shipping & handling (@ $4.00 1ST item)	$
($2.00 each additional item)	$
Total	$

Please make check payable to
MINDFUL LIVING PRODUCTIONS

Name: ____

Address: ____

____

____

Phone Number (_____)___________

PLEASE MAIL ORDER FORM AND CHECK TO:
Mindful Living Productions
647 Washington Blvd. #3
Oak Park, IL 60302.

ALLOW TWO WEEKS FOR DELIVERY

For additional information and/or order forms visit
www.mindfullivingproductions.com

Printed in the United States
60399LVS00004B/205-609

9 781598 009484